Contents

Cross-curricular links 4

Introduction 5

1 Maps and mapping 7

2 The island of Barra 17

3 Transport 26

4 Work and land use 35

5 Compare and contrast 44

6 Likes and dislikes 52

7 Places we have visited 61

8 Seaside weather 69

9 Seaside and home 78

10 Past and present 87

11 Around the world 95

Cross-curricular links

Chapter	Geography SoW	History SoW	Literacy framework	Numeracy framework	ICT SoW
1	Unit 3		Y1, Term 3: T22	Y1: Numbers and the number system	Unit 1A
2	Unit 3		KS1 NC Speaking and listening Y1, Term 1: T12, T14 Y1, Term 2: T22		Unit 1B
3	Unit 3		Y1, Term 2: T25	Y1: Solving problems	Unit 1E
4	Unit 3		Y1, Term 1: T12, T14 Y1, Term 2: T22		Unit 1B
5	Unit 3		Y1, Term 2: T25		Unit 1B
6	Unit 3		Y1, Term 1: T12, T14 Y1, Term 2: T22, T25 Y1, Term 3: T20		Unit 1B
7	Unit 4		Y1, Term 1: T12, T14 Y1, Term 2: T22, T25 Y1, Term 3: T20		Unit 1F
8	Unit 4		Y1, Term 1: T12, T14 Y1, Term 2: T22, T25 Y1, Term 3: T20		Unit 2B
9	Unit 4		KS1 NC Speaking and listening	Y1: Numbers and the number system	Unit 2D
10	Unit 4	Unit 3	Y1, Term 1: T12, T14 Y1, Term 2: T22, T25		Unit 2B
11	Unit 4		Y1, Term 2: T25		Unit 1B

SY 0109208 1

Curious Cactus

Islands and seasides

David Flint

HOPSCOTCH
EDUCATIONAL PUBLISHING

Curriculum Focus series

Geography

History

Toys Key Stage 1
Famous Events Key Stage 1
Famous People Key Stage 1
Invaders Key Stage 2
Tudors Key Stage 2

Geography

Islands and Seasides Key Stage 1
The Local Area Key Stage 1

Science

Ourselves Key Stage 1
Animals, Plants and Habitats: Key Stage 1
Materials: Key Stage 1

Published by Hopscotch Educational Publishing Ltd,
Unit 2, The Old Brushworks, 56 Pickwick Road,
Corsham, Wilts SN13 9BX
Tel: 01249 701701

© 2004 Hopscotch Educational Publishing

Written by David Flint
Linked ICT activities by Michelle Singleton
Series design by Blade Communications
Illustrated by Martin Cater
Cover illustration by Susan Hutchison
Printed by Clintplan, Southam

David Flint hereby asserts his moral right to be identified
as the author of this work in accordance with the
Copyright, Designs and Patents Act, 1988.

ISBN 1-904307-51-5

All rights reserved. This book is sold subject to the
condition that it shall not, by way of trade or otherwise,
be lent, hired out or otherwise circulated without the
publisher's prior consent in any form of binding or cover
other than that in which it is published and without a
similar condition, including this condition, being imposed
upon the subsequent purchaser.

No part of this publication may be reproduced, stored in
a retrieval system, or transmitted, in any form or by any
means, electronic, mechanical, photocopying, recording
or otherwise, without the prior permission of the
publisher, except where photocopying for educational
purposes within the school or other educational
establishment that has purchased this book is expressly
permitted in the text.

Introduction

Curriculum Focus: Islands and Seasides helps to make geography fun and real by giving you (especially if you do not have much geographical background) the materials and support that you need to plan and teach exciting and interesting lessons.

The chapters in this book are based on the QCA exemplar scheme of work for geography at Key Stage 1 and each chapter equips you with the ideas, skills and knowledge to deliver the full range of geography at this key stage.

This book gives you a clear approach to teaching geographical ideas and to planning work for your classes, including:

- background information that includes illustrations
- ideas for introducing and developing the lesson
- differentiated photocopiable activity sheets to support individual and group work.

Islands and seasides are exciting aspects of geography for young children. The intention is to encourage children to look further afield than their own immediate environment and to acquire some basic understanding of what more 'distant' places are like, in terms of similarities and differences.

This book also provides an ideal opportunity to develop a range of ideas and skills, some of which are unique to geography (such as map skills) and some of which are general educational skills (such as description and analysis).

In investigating islands and seasides, this book uses the QCA unit 'An island home', which itself centres upon a series of books by Mairi Hedderwick that deal with the mythical Scottish island of Struay. This book uses the same approach, but also brings the focus onto real examples of Scottish islands such as Barra (which is very similar to Struay).

Another key feature of this book is the way in which it encourages children to think about places and people's lives that may not be immediately local to them. Chapters 4 and 5 deal with aspects of farming and rural life, which may contain both similarities and differences to the children's own local area. This aspect of broadening the children's knowledge and understanding of the world is further developed in Chapter 6, which uses the real Caribbean island of Dominica to show how it, too, has both similarities and differences to local examples. Chapter 7 focuses on places children have visited and this then leads into a study of seaside places in Chapters 8 to 11. The chapters on seaside places again make comparison with the children's home environments and take them further afield to seaside places around the world. They cover the QCA unit 'Going to the seaside'. In addition, the cross-curricular nature of education at this key stage is reinforced by incorporating a study of seaside places in the past as well as in the present.

The material in each chapter is designed to be used flexibly, and not necessarily consecutively with the whole class. It is recognised that many teachers of children of this age prefer to organise their classes so that after the teacher's initial input, different groups work on different activities.

Curriculum Focus: Islands and Seasides recognises that there will be different levels of attainment among children and that their developing reading skills will require different levels of support using individual and group work. To help teachers provide activities that meet the needs of their class, each chapter contains three photocopiable sheets based on the same material, but for children with different levels of attainment. This means that the whole class can take part in a similar activity.

Activity sheet 1 in each chapter is intended for lower-attaining children. Activity sheet 2 should be suitable for most children while Activity sheet 3 challenges higher-attaining children.

Mapping skills

'History is about chaps and geography is about maps,' is an old saying among teachers that still has a great deal of validity. Children meet and see maps and plans in all of their everyday lives, from the plan of the play area showing where to find the swings, slide and climbing frame, to the map of the supermarket showing where to find frozen foods, fresh meat and vegetables. We often assume that children see the same things on a map or plan as adults see, but this is often not the case. So one of the main purposes of geography is to help them to learn to 'read' maps in the same way as they develop literacy skills in reading text. In fact, the skill of using, making and reading maps, called 'graphicacy' or 'visual literacy', ranks alongside traditional literacy and numeracy in terms of children's development. However, graphicacy has never been afforded the importance and time that have been devoted to literacy and numeracy. One of the purposes of this series of *Curriculum Focus* books is to help to rectify this neglect. Children need to be taught how to read a map. It is not a particularly difficult skill and it can involve games and fun activities. One of the problems with the teaching of map skills is that it has to be taught by teachers who themselves are probably not geographers and who may be worried about their own map reading abilities. If this is you, please don't worry – teaching map skills is simple, enjoyable and fun for teachers and for children. These books will show you how to do it in easy steps.

The QCA units of work in geography form the basis of these books. These units of work are extremely useful with their detailed learning objectives and suggested teaching activities. However, many of the units contain references to the development of map skills, such as 'Locate Scotland and the Western Isles on a map,' (Unit 3, An island home), without showing how these skills are to be acquired. These books will help to fill this gap, starting with Chapter 1 on how to build up a series of activities to develop map skills.

Maps and mapping

CHAPTER 1

TEACHERS' NOTES

This book starts with this chapter on ways to develop map skills because they lie at the heart of geography. The intention is to help you and the children get a flying start in understanding geography and how it works. You may want to refer back to these notes and the lesson in this chapter from time to time as you work through other chapters, to remind the children of some of the skills they have acquired. This will help them when they come to use or draw maps in later activities. You will find yourself revisiting Chapter 1 as you work with the children throughout the year.

Work on developing map skills should permeate all aspects of geography, so that children see maps as an integral part of any study, whether the place be local or distant. The development of their map skills is an ongoing process that starts in nursery and continues throughout their lives.

Some basic rules about developing map skills

First of all, there are two big don'ts:

- Please don't start the first lesson on map skills with 'Today we are studying geography and so I want you all to draw a map of your route from home to school.'
- And please don't start the next lesson with 'Next we are going to draw a plan of the classroom.'

These are very difficult activities for adults, let alone children. It is really important that children do not find that they fail in their first activity related to geography. The development of map skills should be fun, enjoyable and, above all, easy. It is important to differentiate the activities so that all the children can see that they are succeeding in map reading from the very first lesson. One interesting finding from recent research is that children who may not be very successful in traditional literacy and numeracy can be extremely successful in terms of map skills, and this may help to motivate all the children in the group.

So the basic rules for developing map skills are as follows:

- Keep it simple.
- Make it fun.
- Use lots of games.
- Avoid overly-detailed and complex maps.
- Build in success.
- Use lots of picture maps in the early stages.
- Avoid complex terminology in the early stages.

Activities for the development of map skills

The key elements needed to draw, use and understand maps are:

- the language of location (using words to describe where things are);
- directions – from left and right to north, south, east and west;
- understanding and using signs and symbols;
- understanding the idea of plan view.

At Key Stage 2 these elements continue and become more complex, and two further elements are added:

- coordinates;
- scale.

Understanding and using signs and symbols

Children are used to seeing and using signs and symbols in their everyday lives. They see road signs on their way to and from school. Many road signs contain no words but use pictures, a diagram or shapes to convey their meaning. Circular signs with a broad red line diagonally across them mean 'do not do' something, such as 'Do not turn right'. Triangular signs advise, such as 'Give way'. Circular road signs with a red band round have to be obeyed, such as speed limit signs. Rectangular signs provide information, such as 'One-way street'.

It is important to help children understand that in the same way, signs and symbols used on a map convey information – a large letter T or a phone symbol (black for public and blue for motoring organisations) shows the location of a telephone box; a square with a cross on top shows a church with a tower. The children do not need to adopt these conventions at the outset. Encourage them to devise and draw their own signs, such as signs for different types of shop – some selling meat, or vegetables, or newspapers. The important points to stress are:

- that the sign looks like what it represents, such as a loaf of bread for a baker's;
- that there is a key, which explains what each sign stands for.

Tell them that the word 'key' is used deliberately because it is the thing that unlocks the whole of the map.

Plan view

This can be one of the more difficult aspects of maps for children to understand. The key elements are:

- Things (objects) look different when we look down on them from above.
- The view from above gives us clues as to what objects are from their shape.
- The view from above makes it hard to see how tall the object is.

The main point is not to expect too much from the children too soon. Introduce them to the idea of plan view gradually, through a series of games and activities. For example, put a variety of objects on the OHP (but hidden from the children) and ask them what they think the objects are; make some cards of objects seen from above and the front and ask the children to match them. Objects for the above two games could include a lamp, a kettle, a cup, a pen and so on.

Note: other mapping activities

The activities in the following lesson plan aim to help the children revise some of the key features of maps – especially plan view and signs and symbols and then to learn how to use grids to locate places.

Curriculum Focus: The Local Area, the sister to this book, contains other useful lesson plans on mapping skills, which address the following objectives:

- to learn some of the language of location;
- to learn the four and eight points of the compass;
- to draw a picture map;
- to learn how to draw and interpret signs and symbols on maps and plans;
- to identify objects from their plan view.

Maps and mapping

LESSON PLAN

> **Geography objectives (Unit 3)**
> • To revise some of the key features of maps – especially plan view and signs and symbols.
> • To use grids to locate places.

Resources

- Generic sheets 1–3 (pages 1–13)
- Activity sheets 1–3 (pages 14–16)
- Marker pens, paper, crayons, pencils and glue or sticky tape

Starting points: *whole class*

Tell the children that they are going to revise some of the maps that they have done in the past. Show them Generic sheet 1 on the OHP or in an enlarged version and explain that it shows a picture and a map of part of a town. The plan and the picture show the same area. Explain that the plan shows the view from above as if you were in an aeroplane looking straight down on the town.

Point to the block of flats in the picture and ask the children what they think the building is. Ask a child to come out and write 'Flats' on the correct shape on the plan. Next, point to the terrace of three houses and ask the children what they think it is. Then ask a child to come out and label it on the plan.

Now point to the fire station in the picture (top right) and ask the children to identify it. This one is more difficult, but if you ask them to focus on the doors at the front someone is likely to spot that it could be a fire or an ambulance station. The tower behind and the fire engine are the clues that it is a fire station rather than an ambulance station. Ask a child to label it on the plan. Repeat this with the flowerbed and the trees on the plan.

Next, work together to devise a set of symbols for a key to show what each building is on the plan, rather than using words each time. Draw the symbols below the plan and name each symbol.

Then show the children Generic sheet 2 on the OHP or in an enlarged version. Explain that these are the shelves in a shop and each shelf is labelled to help us find where things are. So there are some bananas on shelf A1 (be sure to stress the need to give the letter before the number in order to get the children into good habits for when they come to number grids only).

Ask the children, 'What is on shelf B3?' (grapes). Next ask the children to give the references for:

- the apples (A3);
- the carrots (C3);
- the cucumber (C1);
- the cabbage (A2).

Explain that we use a grid to help us find places and things. Next show the children Generic sheet 3 on the OHP or in an enlarged version. Explain that it is another grid that we use to help us find where things are. Ask the children:

- Where is the hat? (B2)
- Where is the ball? (E4)
- Where is the umbrella? (C5)
- Where is the star? (A3)
- Where is the black square? (D1)
- Where is the triangle? (D5)

Now tell the children that they are going to look at some more grids, which will help them to locate things.

Group activities

Activity sheet 1

This sheet is aimed at children who can recognise the pictures of items and who can use a simple letter/number grid. They may need to be reminded that they should give the letter reference first and the number second. The children are given one example, which you may want to go through with them before they start the activity. They have to give the letter/number reference for 14 items in the grid. They can choose which 14 items they wish.

Activity sheet 2

This sheet is aimed at children who are able to use a letter/number grid quite well and who can recognise the shape of eastern England. They have one example of how to give the reference for a town (Cromer K7). They have to give the references for five towns and then use an atlas to help them mark and name three more towns in the correct squares on the map. If there is time, they add other towns to the map.

Activity sheet 3

This sheet is aimed at more able children who understand the idea of a letter/number grid and who are familiar with the map of eastern England. They have to give the references for five towns and then use an atlas to identify the towns with given coordinates marked only with black dots and name them on their map. They also have to mark and name five towns on the map.

Plenary session

Share some of the grids, emphasising the ways in which they help us to locate places and things accurately. Point out that in some maps there are no letters along the bottom of the map but just another set of numbers. Ask why this might be a problem (because it is confusing). Explain that this is why you have been stressing that the letter is always given first. In the same way as in an all-letter grid, the numbers along the bottom are always given first, then the numbers up the side.

Ideas for support

Help the children to understand maps and coordinates by using a series of bookshelves in the classroom. Label each shelf with a number – 1, 2, 3 – and divide each into two or more with pieces of card. Then label each column A, B and so on. Place toys on the shelves in some of the spaces and talk to the children about giving the address for each toy. Then use the letter/number grid to give them addresses for each toy – for example, the doll is in A1; the drum is in B2.

Ideas for extension

Children who are able to use simple letter/number grids can easily progress to using all-number grids. In the first instance, use a relatively small grid of about six or eight squares. Use numbers for the base line that start with, say, 21, 22 and so on, and use numbers for the side that are quite different, such as 65, 66, 67 and so on. Follow the same path as earlier by placing shapes in the grid such as diamonds, circles and stars, and ask the children to give their references. Stress the importance of giving the first set of numbers from along the base and the second set from up the side. Point out that in Ordnance Survey maps the numbers always increase from the bottom left-hand corner. As they become more proficient, use larger and more complicated grids, but try to avoid using the same sets of numbers along the bottom and the side (that is, both numbered 21, 22, 23, 24 and so on) as this tends to confuse children.

Linked ICT activities

You will need access to the program 'My World 2' and the file within this program called 'Maketown'. Show the children how to use the program by dragging and dropping the different sized roads onto the screen, creating different paths and roads. The roads can also be turned to face different directions. Add the different symbols and objects provided in the program to the road scene and begin to create a town or village by adding buildings, trees, houses and so on. Look at the area around the school and try to recreate the roads around the school building. Using the writing tool, show the children how they can add road names to the roads and labels for the buildings.

If you have a whiteboard this activity could be carried out with the whole class. The children could work together labelling the streets and adding the different objects to the scene. Equally, this activity will work as an independent activity for the children to create their own scene.

Maps and mapping

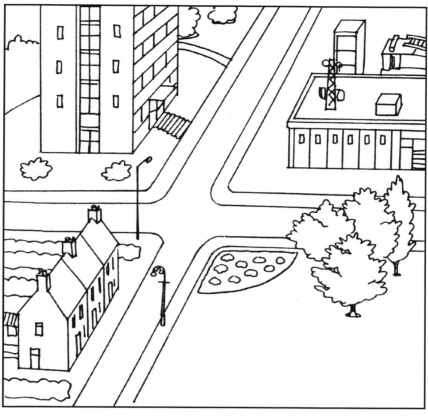

Maps and mapping

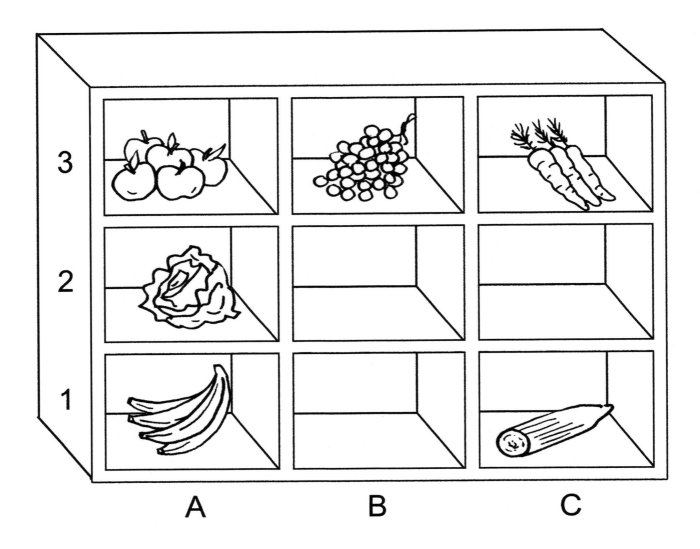

Maps and mapping

Name _____

Maps and mapping

Look at the grid below. The kite is in square A3. On the back of this sheet, give the references and names of 14 other objects.

	A	B	C	D
5	post box	pond	telephone	cup
4	guitar	kettle	train	piano
3	kite	fork	television	clock
2	sheep	cow	telephone box	tree
1	horse	computer	jug	fish

14   CURRICULUM FOCUS • ISLANDS AND SEASIDES

Maps and mapping

Look at the grid below. The town of Cromer is in square K7.

Give the references for:

Leicester   Luton   Hull   Boston   Derby

Use an atlas to help you mark these towns with a red dot on the map and name them:

Northampton   Nottingham   Grimsby

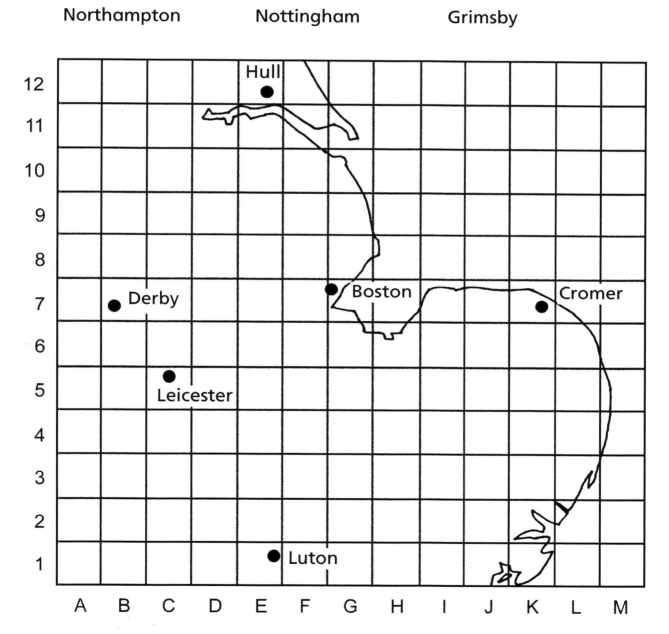

Name _____

Maps and mapping

Look at the grid below. The town of Cromer is in square K7.

Give the references for:

    Leicester   Luton   Hull   Boston   Derby

Use an atlas to label the towns shown in squares K2, B12, A11, B10 and E9.

Use an atlas to help you mark these towns with a red dot on the map and name them:

Northampton   Nottingham   Grimsby   Norwich   Coventry

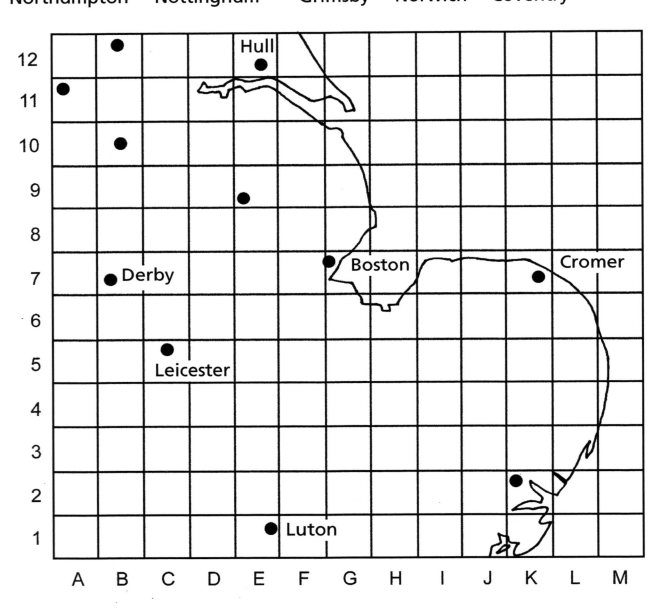

The island of Barra

CHAPTER 2

TEACHERS' NOTES

Barra is a good example of a remote island, like the imaginary island of Struay in the *Katie Morag* books. Barra is a small, relatively remote island with a population of 1300 off the west coast of Scotland.

It is linked to the mainland by ferry and air services from Oban.

Barra is typical of many nearby islands in the way in which its population has declined over the last 100 years. People have gone in search of better paid jobs in more accessible locations on the mainland, or even abroad. The loss of young people has been particularly severe, and has led to the closure or reduction of some services. Physical conditions restrict the scale and economic viability of farming. It is cold, windy and wet for many months of the year. There are few alternative sources of employment. Fishing is declining in line with EU quotas, and tourism provides an income for relatively few people in the short summers. However, the island does provide a beautiful environment, much loved by its remaining inhabitants who guard it with a fierce loyalty.

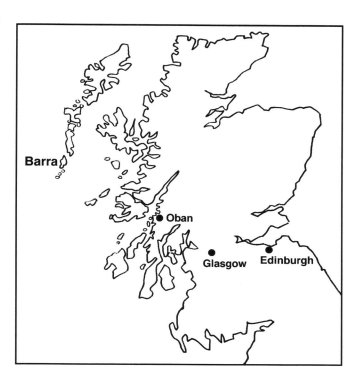

LESSON PLAN

The island of Barra

Geography objectives (Unit 3)
• To identify the physical and human features of a place.
• To learn how an island is different from the mainland.

Resources

• Generic sheets 1–3 (pages 20–22)
• Activity sheets 1–3 (pages 23–25)
• Glue or sticky tape
• A map of north-west Scotland from teachers' notes on page 17
• Words from the word bank on Generic sheet 1 (page 20) written onto separate cards

Starting points: *whole class*

Tell the children that they are going to look at islands and coasts. Show them Generic sheet 1 on an OHP or in an enlarged version. Talk about what they can see in the picture. Point out the sea and the islands and stick the word 'islands' in an appropriate place on the picture. Encourage them to identify other features in the picture and invite them to come out to stick the words on the picture.

Ask the children to tell you which are physical features (islands, sea, beach, cliffs) and which are human features (harbour, boat, cottage). Write these words on the board under appropriate headings.

Next explain to the children that they are going to look at one island in particular – the island of Barra. Use the map from page 17 to locate Barra off the west coast of Scotland. Show the children Generic sheet 2 on an OHP or in an enlarged version and ask questions such as:

• In which part of the island does the ferry arrive – north, south, east or west? (south)
• In which part of the island is the airfield? (north)
• In which part of the island is the main hotel? (west)
• How is the island different from mainland Scotland? (It is surrounded by water.)
• What do you think are the problems of being surrounded by water when people have to go to hospital in an emergency? (They have to go by air.)

Use the three pictures on Generic sheet 3 to help the children get a realistic idea of what life in Barra is like. The pictures show the harbour at Barra, the ferry leaving Oban and planes landing on the beach. You could discuss with the children some problems associated with living on islands like Barra – for example, the need to use a ferry or travel by air. You could also talk about the problems of communication between an island and the mainland.

Tell the children that they are now going to study an island and its features.

Group activities

Activity sheet 1
This sheet is aimed at children who need more support. They can identify a range of physical and human features found on an island. They have to write the words from the word bank in the correct places on the picture. Then, on the back of the sheet, they have to draw a picture of themselves arriving on the island by boat or helicopter.

Activity sheet 2
This sheet is aimed at children who can work independently. They can recognise the main physical and human features of a place and are familiar with the four main points of the compass. They have to label the main features of the island from a word bank, then draw features in the centre and on each side of the island. Ask them to draw a picture of a person being airlifted to hospital.

Activity sheet 3
This sheet is aimed at more able children. They can easily recognise human and physical features of an island and are familiar with the four main points of the compass. They have to label the key features on the picture and draw in new ones using the compass reference points. On the back of the sheet, they have to draw two pictures showing the process of airlifting a patient to hospital on the mainland.

Plenary session

Share the responses to the activity sheets and recap the main physical and human features of the island. Ask the children to explain how the island is different from the mainland. Talk about the problems of living on an island, such as the need to use the ferry or travel by air for anything that isn't available on the island. Talk about how the weather can disrupt travel.

Ideas for support

Some children may have difficulty in relating the words to the key sections of the picture so, starting with the harbour, talk about how it is protected from the winds and high waves. Then discuss the ferry boat which is the link to the mainland. Move left to focus on the beach which spreads out from the land. This should give the children a good start in understanding the rest of the picture.

Ask the children to draw some pictures to accompany the following story.

- One windy day, Ali and Amee went playing on the beach near the cliffs.
- Suddenly they looked up, and the tide had come in. They were trapped.
- Luckily, a man walking his dog along the cliffs heard their cries for help.
- He phoned the coastguard.
- The lifeboat came and rescued them.

Ideas for extension

Introduce children to the eight points of the compass. Give them a clean copy of the picture of the island from Activity sheet 3. This time ask them to draw a range of features using the eight points of the compass, such as:

- a road between the two villages which goes via the south-west of the island;
- a hotel on the south-east coast of the island;
- a patch of trees on the north-west corner of the island;
- a lighthouse off the south-east corner of the island.

Ask the children to draw pictures and write sentences to tell the story of a day trip in a small boat from the island. A storm blows up and the boat sinks, so the people have to be rescued by lifeboat and helicopter.

Linked ICT activities

Using a word processing program with a word bank, such as 'Talking Write Away', 'Textease' or 'Clicker 4', create a word bank containing words from Generic sheet 1 and other high frequency words which may be useful for the children. Show them how to insert the words in the word bank as part of their writing on the page. Use the pictures on Generic sheet 3 as a starting point, and from the discussions which you have had with the children about living in Barra, ask them to write a sentence to match each of the pictures, using the word bank to help them.

Print out the sentences and cut them into strips. Ask the children to write their names on the back of each sentence strip and then pass the sentences to a friend with the pictures. See if the children can then match the right sentences with the pictures. If they can't see which sentences should match the pictures talk to them about what they need to add to the sentences so that it is very clear which pictures the sentences should match.

The island of Barra

WORD BANK

islands   harbour   boat   cliffs

sea   helicopter   mainland   cottage   beach

The island of Barra

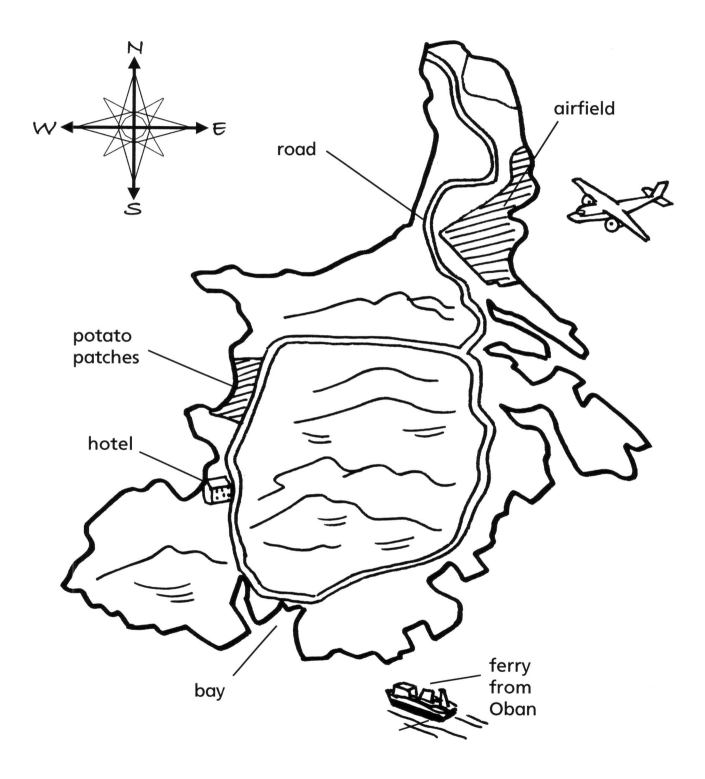

road

airfield

potato patches

hotel

bay

ferry from Oban

ST. MARY'S UNIVERSITY COLLEGE
A COLLEGE OF THE QUEEN'S UNIVERSITY OF BELFAST

The island of Barra

Name _____

An island

Write the words from the word bank in the correct places on the picture.

WORD BANK			
mountain	island	sea	beach
cliff	river	harbour	road
mainland	ferry boat		

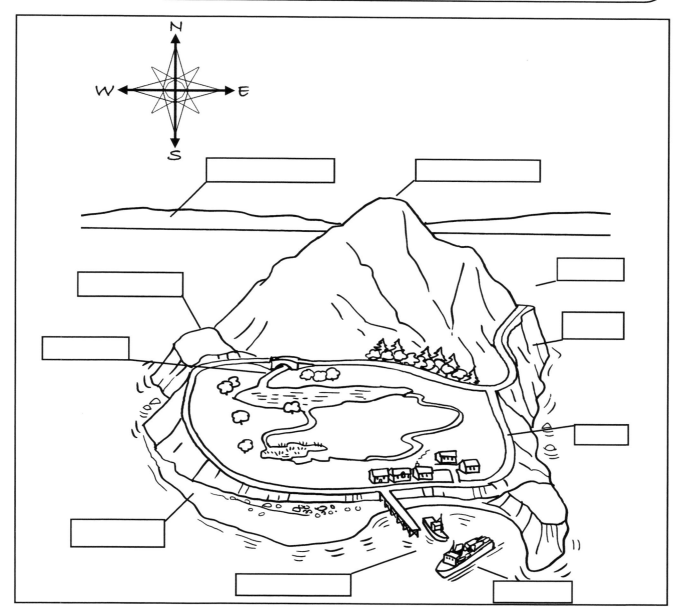

On the back of this sheet, draw a picture of yourself arriving on this island by boat or helicopter.

Name _____

An island

Write the correct name from the word bank next to each arrow.

WORD BANK

mountain	island	sea	beach	ferry boat
cliff	lake	harbour	mainland	

Next draw:

- a road between the two villages;
- an airfield in the north;
- three fields to grow crops on the east side of the island;
- a hotel on the south side of the island;
- some trees on the west side of the island.

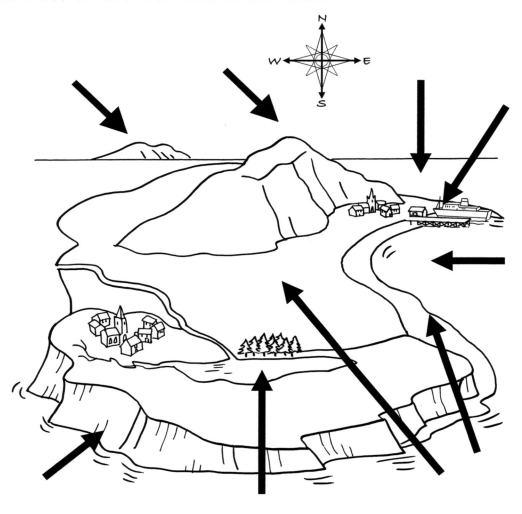

Name _____

An island

Label the key features shown in the picture.

Then draw:

- a road between the two villages;
- some trees on the north-west side of the island;
- a fishing boat in the harbour;
- three fields for crops on the south-east side of the island;
- a hotel on the south side of the island.

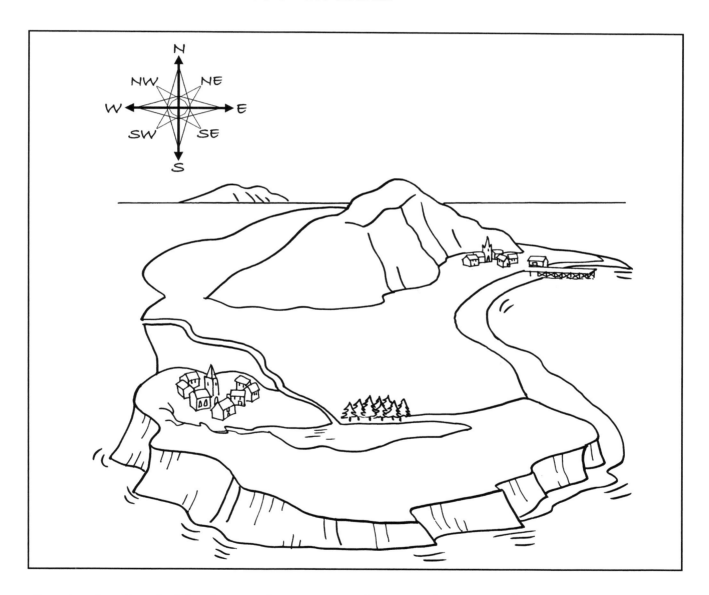

On the back of this sheet, draw two pictures showing the process of airlifting a patient to hospital on the mainland.

Transport

The role of transport

Transport is vital to the economy of a country and to the quality of people's lives. It is necessary to move goods and people around a country and between countries. It also helps to increase the wealth of a country and the standard of living of the people. However, recently people have begun to realise that transport is becoming more and more expensive, that it causes conflict between groups of people, and that it creates environmental problems.

Each type of transport has its own advantages and disadvantages as the table on Generic sheet 1 summarises (see page 29).

When choosing the most appropriate type of transport for the movement of goods or people, there are several factors to consider:

- Time – how long will the journey take?
- Distance – how far is the journey?
- Cost – what will the cost of the journey be?
- Frequency – how often will the journey be made?

Transport and islands

Because of their situation, transport is vital to island communities. In most cases transport is centred on the use of water transport because it is ideal for moving cars, vans and lorries, as well as the heavy goods people need, such as new bathroom suites or furniture. Regular ferry services are the lifelines which connect islands like Barra with communities on the mainland. Air transport is important for items such as mail, newspapers and people in a hurry, but there are many things that can only go by sea.

Road, rail, water and air transport in the UK

In 1900 nearly all of Britain's goods were moved by rail or water. By 2000 over 80 per cent of UK goods and 95 per cent of passenger movements were by road.

Road

The biggest single advantage of road transport is that it offers door-to-door journeys with no

changes. Cars are being used more and more for journeys to work, shopping, holidays and recreation because they are relatively cheap to use, especially over short distances. Lorries have become more specialised in the cargoes they carry. Now goods loaded at a UK factory can be sent all over Europe without having to be transferred to another vehicle or type of transport. The growing popularity of road transport, especially cars, has created problems such as traffic jams, accidents, pollution and a decline in public transport. People who do not have access to a car are disadvantaged.

Rail

Compared with road transport, rail travel avoids traffic jams, causes less pollution, is cheaper and quicker over relatively long distances and is safer and more comfortable. Despite these advantages, the amount of goods and the number of passengers carried by rail are declining in comparison with road transport. One of the main reasons for this is the time spent travelling to and from stations, and also the need to transfer from one type of transport to another. Rail is ideal for carrying heavy, bulky goods such as coal and cement.

Water

Water transport is ideal for moving heavy, bulky objects or goods that are of relatively low value, such as coal, iron ore and timber. In the UK, water transport (by rivers and canals) lost its popularity when the railways appeared, improving speed and therefore reducing costs. However, in recent years there has been renewed interest in rivers and canals, particularly for leisure and recreation. Many people now sail narrow boats (older converted barges) or modern motor cruisers along the networks of rivers and canals, which have been renovated.

Air

Air transport is ideal for moving people and perishable goods over quite long distances and to relatively remote places, such as islands. The British Isles are made up of hundreds of islands, both large and small, from the Isle of Wight to the tiny islands of Scotland, such as Barra. Air transport is vital in maintaining links between these islands and the rest of the UK and the world.

Transport

LESSON PLAN

Geography objective (Unit 3)
- To identify types of transport.

Resources

- A large copy (A3 or bigger) of the map of the Isle of Struay from any of the *Katie Morag* books
- Generic sheets 2 and 3 (pages 30 and 31)
- Activity sheets 1–3 (pages 32–34)
- A copy of *Katie Morag delivers the mail* by Mairi Hedderwick (Collins, 1984)
- Scissors and glue

Starting points: *whole class*

Tell the children that they are going to look at pictures that show different ways to move things. One at a time, show them the pictures on Generic sheet 2. Ask them what each vehicle is and what it carries.

Tell the children that you are going to sort the pictures in some way. Sort them into two groups, such as transport on land and transport in the air. Ask the children to guess how they have been sorted. You could ask them for other ways to sort the vehicles, such as by size or by speed.

Now keep Generic sheet 2 on display and show the children Generic sheet 3. Explain that these are plan views of the vehicles on Generic sheet 2. Ask them to look carefully and to point to which plan matches which vehicle. When they are correct, put coloured ticks or crosses to link pictures and plans.

Next, tell the children that they will be looking at the Isle of Struay and Katie Morag. Show them the large version of the map of the island. Tell them that they are going to look at different types of transport. Some types of transport are used to reach the island, and some to get around on the island.

Read *Katie Morag delivers the mail* to the children. Before you begin, stress the importance of the mail arriving by boat from the mainland. Ask the children to watch out for examples of how people get around on the island (in the text and in the pictures).

Ask questions such as:

- How did Katie deliver the parcels? (on foot)
- How did Grannie get around the island to sort out the parcels? (by tractor)

Tell the children that they are now going to think about the different types of transport used to get to Struay and the different types of transport used on the island.

Group activities

Activity sheet 1

This sheet is aimed at children who need more support. They can recognise different types of transport. They have to distinguish between those types of transport used to reach an island and those used to get around on the island itself. They have to draw the transport in the correct oval. On another sheet of paper, they have to draw a picture of a car, a bus or a bicycle.

Activity sheet 2

This sheet is aimed at children who can work independently. They are familiar with the use of different types of transport. They have to draw the transport in the correct circle. On another sheet of paper, they have to draw a picture of a type of transport used in their local area and write a sentence about other types of transport.

Activity sheet 3

This sheet is aimed at more able children. They are able to recognise the merits of different types of transport. They have to cut out the pictures, sort them into three groups and stick them in the correct circles. They also have to write a few sentences about the types of transport found on the island.

Plenary session

Share the responses to the activity sheets. Recap why transport is restricted on Struay and discuss what problems this creates (how to get people to hospital quickly in an emergency and how to move heavy equipment around the island). Ask the children what the island needs to help get people to hospital quickly (a helicopter).

Ideas for support

Encourage the children to play with toys that represent a range of different types of transport, from bulldozers to helicopters, lorries and buses. Ask the children what each vehicle is used for. Ask them to sort the vehicles into sets and let them choose the sets – for example, on the basis of colour, size or speed. Suggest other ways in which they could sort the toys – for example, those that move on land, on water and in the air.

Ask the children to describe journeys they have made in different forms of transport, from car to bus to plane. Ask them what they liked and what they disliked about the journey. Get them to draw a picture relating to a memorable journey.

Ideas for extension

Ask the children to think about the use of different types of transport for different purposes. You could set them a challenge such as this:

Challenge
Move some perishable flowers from Jersey (in the Channel Islands) to Birmingham as quickly as possible.

Then ask the children to suggest the type of transport that is most suitable.

Type of transport most suitable
Aircraft: this form of transport is fast. Although air transport is expensive, people will pay high prices for fresh flowers.

Other problems you could set are:

- move part of a motorway bridge from Sheffield to Southampton;
- deliver expensive diamonds to Edinburgh from London;
- move 100 tonnes of timber from a forest in Scotland to a pulp and paper mill in Northern Ireland;
- move new furniture from Liverpool to the Isle of Man.

Ask the children to draw a series of pictures that show someone travelling by a range of different types of transport. This person could start from home by car, transfer at a port to a ferry, then catch a plane and finally hire a bicycle to reach a beach in a remote part of a Scottish island. They could then use a rowing boat to cross a lake to reach a cottage on an island in the middle of the lake.

Linked ICT activities

Talk to the children about the different ways they might travel near to their homes. Discuss with them when they might travel by train, car or aeroplane. Talk to them about the different ways they get to school. Some might walk, some might go by taxi and others might travel by bus. Working with the whole class, ask the children to write their names on pieces of card. Pin pictures/photographs on the wall in front of the children showing the different ways in which they get to school; for example, a child walking, a school bus and so on. Ask the children to put their name card under the picture that shows how they get to school.

Using the program 'Counter for Windows' and the file 'Counter' within this program, create a list of the different ways in which the children get to school. Count the number of children, for example, who walk to school and add the number to the correct word in the list. Complete the list and show the children how this information can be displayed as a bar chart. Use the chart to ask the children questions such as 'How many children in our class come to school on a bus?'

Transport

	Road	Rail	Air	Water
Speed/time	Fast over short distances and motorways.	Fast over longer distances.	Fastest over long distances.	Slowest.
Distance/cost	Cheap over short distances.	Relatively cheap over longer distances with bulky goods.	Relatively cheap over long distances with light goods.	Cheapest.
Running costs	High cost of building new roads and repairing old ones. Lorries are relatively cheap to buy and run.	High cost of maintaining track and signalling. New and faster trains are expensive.	Large airports are expensive in terms of land; aircraft use lots of expensive fuel.	High cost of port charges. Ships are expensive.
Number of routes	Numerous – from motorways to minor roads.	Mainly limited to freight and passengers between larger cities.	Few international airports.	Few coastal ports. Little inland freight traffic on canals.
Congestion	Heavy in towns and some main roads. Daily and seasonal peaks.	No congestion on most routes except commuter lines.	Very little – some at airports at peak holiday times.	Very little.
Weather	Fog and ice cause accidents. Snow blocks roads.	Very little affected by bad weather.	Fog stops some plane movements.	Storms affect coasts and ferries.
Volume of freight	Small amount.	Greater amount, especially heavy, bulky goods.	Medium amount, especially light, high value and perishable goods.	Greater amount, especially heavy, bulky goods.
Passengers per vehicle	3–4 adults.	Several hundred.	Up to 300 on international flights.	Very few passengers.
Convenience	Door to door.	Town to town.	City to city.	Port to port.
Comfort	Good, though stressful for drivers.	Good over medium distances.	Good over long distances.	Good.
Pollution	Noise and air pollution, acid rain, global warming.	Noise pollution in a few areas.	High noise pollution and some air pollution.	Very little (until an oil tanker sinks).

Transport

Petrol tanker

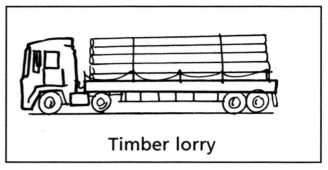
Timber lorry

Double-decker bus

Milk float

Cement lorry

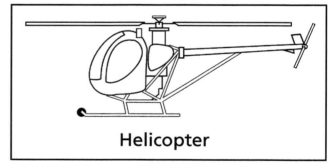
Helicopter

Car

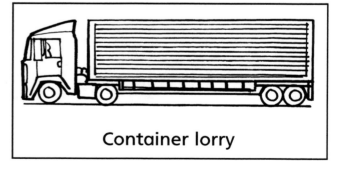
Container lorry

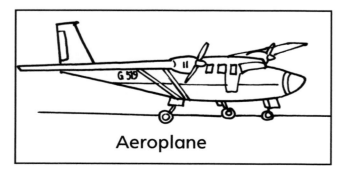
Aeroplane

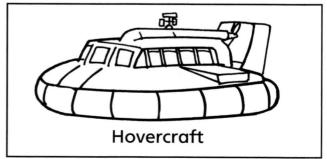
Hovercraft

Transport

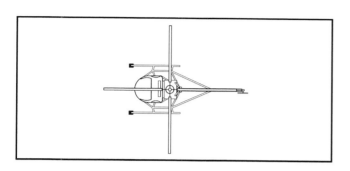

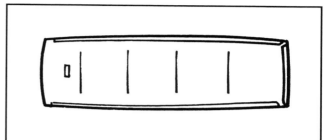

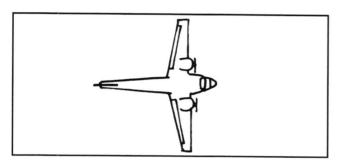

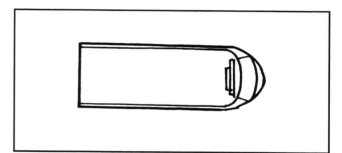

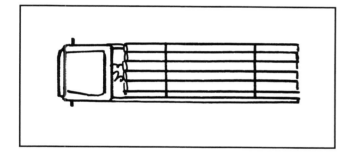

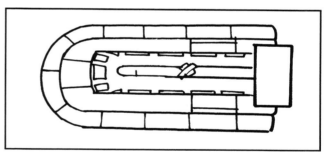

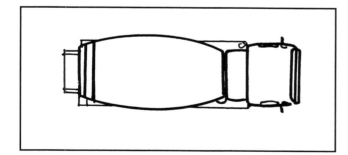

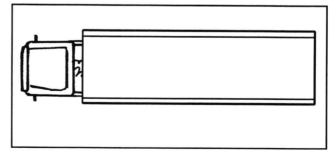

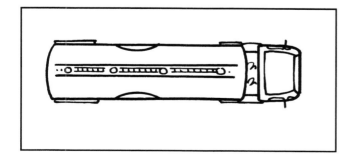

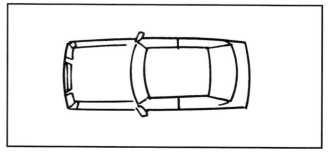

Name _____

Transport

Look at the pictures of transport.
Draw those that could be used to get to Struay in the correct oval.
Draw those that could be used to get around on the island in the correct oval.

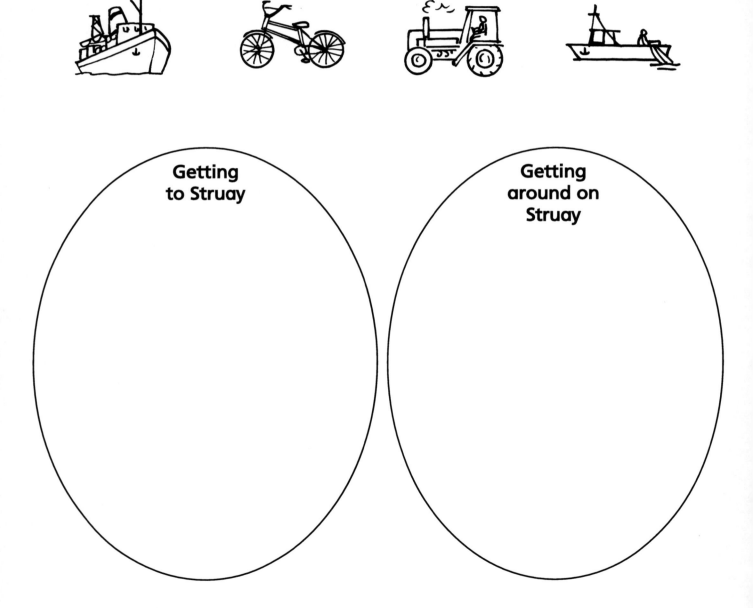

Getting
to Struay

Getting
around on
Struay

On another sheet of paper, draw a picture of you in a car, on a bus
or on a bicycle.

Transport

Look at the pictures.
Draw those that could be used to get to Struay in the correct oval.
Draw those that could be used to get around on the island in the correct oval.

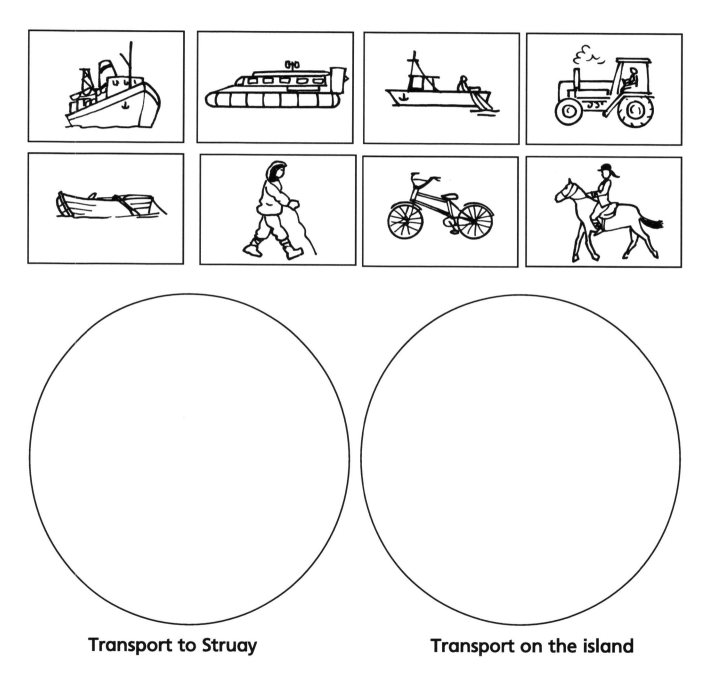

Transport to Struay   **Transport on the island**

On another sheet of paper, draw a picture of a type of transport that can be used where you live. Write a sentence about other types of transport.

Transport

Draw three circles on a separate sheet of paper.
Label the first circle 'Transport to Struay'.
Label the second circle 'Transport on the island'.
Label the third circle 'Moving things in the UK'.

Cut out the pictures below. Stick those that show how to get to Struay in the first circle. Stick those that show how to get around on the island in the second circle. Stick those that show how to move things in the UK in the third circle.

Write some sentences about the types of transport found on Struay.

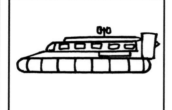

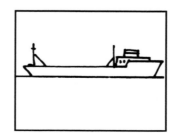

Work and land use

CHAPTER 4

TEACHERS' NOTES

Many Scottish islands, in common with other islands, have experienced very mixed fortunes over the last few decades in terms of jobs, government help, population change and the effects of all these factors on land use.

Population change

In the 1970s and 1980s, remote islands like the fictional Struay, or more realistically Barra and the Hebrides, experienced a steady loss of population. The reasons for this population decline were:

- The lack of local jobs, especially for young people.
- Most available jobs were in farming and fishing and these were declining industries.
- Fishing was hard, dangerous work and, as falling quotas were imposed by the EU to preserve fish stocks, fishing fleets declined and boats were scrapped.
- Farming in western Scotland is very difficult – the islands have very thin, acid soil so plants do not grow well; the climate is cold and wet in winter and warm and wet in summer; crops do not ripen easily; the main type of farming is rearing sheep and cattle.
- The local services available are poor – many remote areas lack bus services, libraries, shops, schools and pubs and as people begin to leave the islands and highlands, so even more of these services become uneconomic and are forced to close, creating a downward spiral.

Once this pattern of population decline is established it becomes difficult to break. One of the main problems is that the people leaving the islands are the younger, more progressive elements of the population. The result is that the population of remote rural areas tends to be the older, less mobile elements of the population. With few children, schools soon close.

The population turnaround (counter-urbanisation)

However, the long-term population decline of areas such as Barra in north-west Scotland began to change in the 1980s and 1990s. Fewer people left and some people began to move in. The reasons for this population turnaround were as follows:

- The growth, development and publicity given to the development of tourism in the area by Highlands and Islands Enterprise – many more people started to visit the area as part of a tour of Scotland.
- Some people from Glasgow and Edinburgh (and a few from the rest of the UK) retired to north-west Scotland; they were looking for peace and quiet in a scenic area, and decided that this area had all these features.
- Other people from the rest of Scotland bought old cottages and barns and renovated them as holiday homes; these second homes provided work for local builders, and they were occupied at weekends and for longer periods during the summer.
- People discovered new ways of working from home using computers and telecommunications, so more people were able to do most of their work anywhere and send the results via email, fax or telephone; consequently some of these people have chosen to live in quiet, remote areas with great scenery and high air quality, such as north-west Scotland.
- Tours have been organised to islands like Barra for specialist groups, such as geologists, birdwatchers and painters. All such groups need places to stay and eat plus a range of other services that have given a boost to the local economy.
- In yet other areas cheap housing has been built specifically to attract young families with children. As more such families move into an area so the local school is able to grow and prosper.
- Highlands and Islands Enterprise helped local communities to support themselves by giving grants to help build new community centres in places like Barra; other grants or loans are available to help people set up businesses such as fish farming or the development of local bus services.

Thinking about the farming system

It is useful for children to think about farming from an early age. They are often unaware that eggs come from chickens or milk from cows or goats. They need to understand where their food comes from. In order to do this, they might usefully think of farming as a system with inputs, processes and outputs.

The inputs include the weather (sunshine, rainfall, temperature) and the soil as well as the costs of labour, transport, machinery, seeds, livestock, fertilisers and buildings that all go into farming.

The processes are growing crops and rearing animals and storing the produce.

The outputs are crops, animal products (milk, meat, cheese, eggs, yoghurt) and the animals themselves.

In this way, as children get older, they will have a systems framework into which they will be able to fit the additional knowledge they acquire.

The example below shows a typical farm system for an arable farm in the Vale of York.

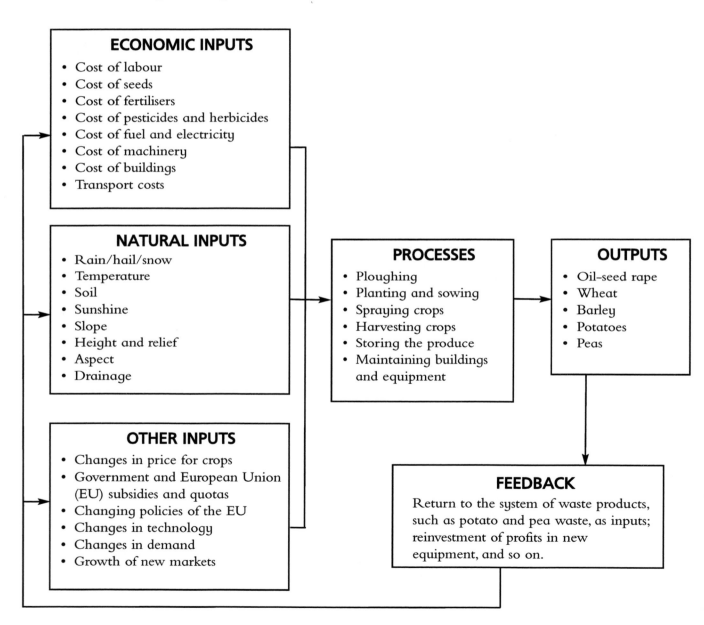

ECONOMIC INPUTS
- Cost of labour
- Cost of seeds
- Cost of fertilisers
- Cost of pesticides and herbicides
- Cost of fuel and electricity
- Cost of machinery
- Cost of buildings
- Transport costs

NATURAL INPUTS
- Rain/hail/snow
- Temperature
- Soil
- Sunshine
- Slope
- Height and relief
- Aspect
- Drainage

OTHER INPUTS
- Changes in price for crops
- Government and European Union (EU) subsidies and quotas
- Changing policies of the EU
- Changes in technology
- Changes in demand
- Growth of new markets

PROCESSES
- Ploughing
- Planting and sowing
- Spraying crops
- Harvesting crops
- Storing the produce
- Maintaining buildings and equipment

OUTPUTS
- Oil-seed rape
- Wheat
- Barley
- Potatoes
- Peas

FEEDBACK
Return to the system of waste products, such as potato and pea waste, as inputs; reinvestment of profits in new equipment, and so on.

Work and land use

LESSON PLAN

Geography objectives (Unit 3)
- To learn what work people do.
- To learn how land and buildings are used.

Resources
- Generic sheets 1 and 2 (pages 39 and 40)
- Activity sheets 1–3 (pages 41–43)
- A large copy (A3 or bigger) of the map of the Isle of Struay from any of the *Katie Morag* books
- A set of coloured marker pens

Starting points: *whole class*

Tell the children that they are going to start by looking at the map of Struay. Show the map and use it to ask questions such as:

- Who lives in the post office? (Mr and Mrs McColl)
- Who else lives on the island? (Grannie, Katie Morag, Mrs Bayview, Lady Artist, Mr MacMaster)
- What work do they do? (Grannie is a farmer; Mrs Bayview takes in guests; Lady Artist paints; Mr MacMaster is a farmer; Mr and Mrs McColl run the post office.)

Next show the children Generic sheet 1 on an OHP or in an enlarged version. Explain that this is a picture of part of an island similar to Struay. Ask them to list all the different ways in which the land is used. Ask a child to come out and write these on the correct places on the picture:

- forests (wood products)
- farmland (crops)
- farmland (animals)
- farm house
- mountain (holidays)
- orchard (fruit farming)
- land (holidays)

Then show them Generic sheet 2 on an OHP or in an enlarged version. Explain that this is the centre of a town. Ask them to spot all the different ways in which the land is used. Point out the bulleted list, then ask some children to come out to colour:

- the transport land uses in red (bus and train stations and car park)
- the living areas in green (houses, flats)
- the offices in yellow (bank and offices)
- the shops in orange (stores)
- other land uses in blue (church).

Ask what jobs people do in, for example, the transport areas. (Drive buses or trains, sell tickets, sell food and drink, clean and service buses and trains, take money in car parks.)

Tell the children that they are now going to look at the jobs that can be found in the countryside on islands like Struay and the jobs that can be found in towns.

Group activities

Activity sheet 1
This sheet is aimed at children who need more support. They can recognise pictures of different types of job and can distinguish jobs in towns from those in the countryside. They have to colour country jobs in green and town jobs in red. On the back of the sheet, they have to draw pictures of two more town jobs and two more rural jobs.

Activity sheet 2
This sheet is aimed at children who can work independently. They not only recognise that there are some jobs that are unique to towns and some that are unique to rural areas, but also understand that some jobs may be common to both. When they divide the pictures into these three groups they may need some help with jobs common to both areas (church, post office, garage). On another sheet of paper they have to draw pictures of two more town jobs, two more rural jobs and two more jobs to be found in both areas.

Activity sheet 3
This sheet is aimed at more able children. They can readily understand the difference between town jobs and rural jobs and understand that some jobs

are common to both areas. They have to sort the pictures into three groups, then add the names of three more jobs to each group.

Plenary session

Share the responses to the activity sheets and talk about other jobs that are found in rural areas, such as fishing. Talk about jobs only found in cities and towns, such as driving underground or metro trains or supervising car parks. Then talk briefly about jobs common to both areas, such as garage work, church work and transport work. Explain how some services come to rural areas in vans, such as mobile libraries and even post offices.

Ideas for support

Talk to the children about Activity sheet 1. Ask them to describe what is happening in each picture. Then ask them if the job is likely to be in the countryside or in a town.

Ask the children to draw a picture of a mobile shop that Katie Morag and Grannie could drive around the island, selling fruit, vegetables or even bread to the people of the island.

Ask the children to draw a picture of Katie Morag helping Grannie and Grannie's sheepdogs to round up some sheep, or showing Katie rescuing a lamb that gets stuck in a bog. Talk about the way in which these sorts of activities are part of work in the countryside on islands like Barra.

Ideas for extension

Tell the children that they have to design and paint an advert for the Holiday House on Struay. The owner wants to attract people from the rest of the UK to come and stay in the house. Talk about the things they should show and write to make the area sound attractive, such as beautiful scenery, lovely lochs, beaches, clean air, an opportunity for some peace and quiet, and boat trips.

Ask the children to draw a series of two or three pictures to show a family getting on a ferry with their luggage. Then show the ferry in a storm with huge waves and people feeling ill or afraid. Finally, show the people arriving on Struay, battered but safe. Encourage them to write some words to accompany the picture story.

Talk about land use, ie how land is used. In the countryside some land is used for farming, such as grass for the animals or ploughed land for crops. Other land is used in different ways, such as for shops or houses or offices. Ask children to write down all the ways in which land is used in the area near your school.

Linked ICT activities

Talk to the children about what they have already found out about Struay. Using a word processing program with a word bank such as 'Talking Write Away', 'Textease' or 'Clicker 4', tell them that they are going to be a person living on the island. Create a word bank with words that will help them to write about the person they are going to be. If you have a digital camera take a picture of the child and add it to the page. Tell the children they are going to describe who they are and what their job on the island is. Print off their completed text and create a large book containing all the children's work. Give the book the title 'Meet the people of the Isle of Struay'.

Work and land use

HOLIDAY CHALETS

FORESTRY
jfh lhf ldhfldhflhf

Work and land use

Look at the picture. Colour:

- transport land use in red
- living areas in green
- offices in yellow
- shops in orange
- other land uses in blue.

Name _____

Work and land use

Look at the pictures. Some show jobs in the country. Colour these green. Some show jobs in towns. Colour these red. Jobs that could be in either town or country shold be coloured blue.

On the back of this sheet, draw four <u>other</u> pictures, two of jobs in towns and two of jobs in the country.

Work and land use

Cut out the pictures and sort them into three groups. Give these groups the names 'Jobs in towns', 'Jobs in the country' and 'Jobs in both town and country'.

On another sheet of paper, draw pictures of two more jobs in towns, two more jobs in the country and two more jobs that can be found in both town and country.

Name _____

Work and land use

Cut the pictures out and sort them into three groups.
Give the groups names.
Explain why you have chosen these groups, then add the names
of three more jobs to each group.

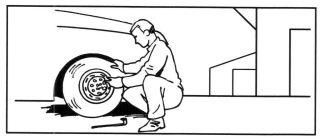

Compare and contrast

Studying the wider world

It is important that children know and understand the ways in which the wider world affects their lives. This should help them to see some similarities and differences between distant places and their own local area. The main reasons for the need to study places that are some distance from the local area are listed below:

- There is a danger of too many local studies within the geography curriculum. Many teachers are very skilled in teaching about the local area and have built up resources that they use to great effect. However, children need to realise the importance of the wider world and its impact on their lives, such as how a decision made in Tokyo might lead to a factory closure and unemployment somewhere in the UK.

- Children have a natural curiosity about distant places and when they see pictures of people and places they want to know what it would be like to live there.

- Many children travel to distant places on holiday (such as the USA, Europe and Australia) and to visit relatives in the Caribbean, India, Pakistan, Canada or Bangladesh. These children need a framework into which they can fit their experiences and geography should provide this.

- Increasingly, issues are global, such as the changes in the 'greenhouse gases' in the atmosphere and consequent rising sea levels. Similarly, the spread of pollution across large areas of the world as a result of accidents, such as the escape of radioactivity from Chernobyl in the Ukraine in 1986, emphasises the importance of a global viewpoint.

- Research suggests that children in primary school are at the most receptive age to avoid stereotyping, so teaching about people and places in distant lands can help to prepare children to be responsible global citizens in the future.

The main pitfalls in teaching about distant places

The dangers of over-generalisation

For example, it may be true that women in a village in Africa have to walk for two hours each day to fetch water from a well, which they then carry home in containers on their heads. However, it is not true to say that Africa is short of water, nor that all African people live in villages.

The dangers of stereotyping

It is fine to study a village in India or Mexico, but it is also important for the children to realise that there are other people in these countries who live in high-rise flats in big cities, with traffic jams, TV and all the 'benefits' of western consumer culture. Try not to give the impression of 'simple people living a simple life', which is patronising and usually not typical.

The dangers of sweeping general solutions to complex problems

Children often see the poverty and problems of the developing world and want to help. They should not be led to believe that there are simple answers, such as birth control or donating more money, to complex problems. Stress that helping people to help themselves is the best direction to move in.

The dangers of painting the lives of people in Africa, Asia or South America as extremely hazardous

The threats from (geographically interesting) hurricanes, earthquakes, droughts and volcanic eruptions are present in some places, but children need to realise that they are not typical of the whole of these continents.

The dangers of the product approach

Avoid studying a distant place in terms only of foods (bananas, coffee, tea) that they export to the UK. This may be a good starting point for a study of a distant place, but avoid suggesting that the people in these places exist only to supply us with bananas, coffee or tea. They are part of cultures and societies equally valuable to those in the UK.

How to approach the study of distant places with children

The big challenge is how to make a distant place 'real'. When children study their local environment, it is very real because they can see it, touch it, smell it and hear it.

- As a starting point, use a child (possibly from another class) who has visited a distant place. Ask them to record what they thought about the place – the weather, food, shops, clothes, houses, work places, games, people, and so on. Then use this recording (plus any photos and video footage) to start a study of a distant place.

- Study small-scale areas. Don't try to cover the whole of Brazil, India or Nigeria, for example. Rather study a village – there are lots of case studies available. Study real named villages and real people in these villages or part of a town. This will help the children to empathise with children living in a distant place.

- Focus on things that children can compare directly with their own experience, such as:

food	getting around
clothing	houses
going to school	shops/supermarkets
getting up	jobs
meal times	roads and traffic
daily routines	landscape

- Use pictures, videos and other supporting aids to help make the place seem real. The internet can be a huge help in terms of finding details of people's lives in distant places. Teachers may want to start by giving children details of organisations such as Oxfam, Christian Aid and Action Aid, who all produce good case studies of life in distant places.
www.oxfam.org.uk
www.christianaid.org.uk
www.actionaid.org.uk
www.actionaidindia.org
www.actionaidpakistan.org
www.allafrica.com
www.africaaction.org

Another possible approach to making things real is to show a product from another country, such as:

- a bunch of bananas
- a coconut
- a mango
- a packet of tea
- a jar of coffee.

Talk to the children about the product and explain that it grew on a plant in a distant part of the world. If possible, show pictures of the plant and the sort of area in which it grew.

Explain that people in that distant place have picked the crop (leaves if it is tea or beans if it is coffee) and then packed it and sent it by lorry to the coast. There, the product will have been loaded onto a ship, to sail to the UK.

Finally, the product will have travelled by lorry to a local supermarket or shop where we can buy it. In the case of tea and coffee, you will need to explain the processing and packaging of the product, which often takes place in the UK before it is distributed to shops and supermarkets.

Then the children can draw a series of pictures to tell the story of how the product gets from where it is grown to the shelves of their local supermarket.

Compare and contrast

Geography objectives (Unit 3)
- To know that the world extends outside their locality.
- To recognise similarities and differences and communicate them.

Resources

- Generic sheet 1 (page 48)
- Activity sheets 1–3 (pages 49–51)
- A large map of the world
- A map of Struay from one of the *Katie Morag* stories
- A marker pen

Starting points: *whole class*

Tell the children that they are going to look at the links between places. In particular, they will look at the links between the UK and the rest of the world. Tell them that one of the most important links is food. Ask questions such as:

- Where do we get oranges from?
- Where do we get peaches from?

Next show the children Generic sheet 1 on an OHP or in an enlarged version. Ask a child to come out and locate Spain on a world map. Together find:

- Africa
- Asia
- Europe
- North America
- South America
- Australia

Explain that we are linked to all the countries on Generic sheet 1 by the food that they grow and sell to us. Explain that some of these places are similar to the local area and some are quite different. They may have different weather (hot and wet in the tropics where bananas are grown; hot and dry in the areas of Algeria where dates are grown). The people may wear different clothes to many people in the UK or their houses may look different. In other places, the people have houses and clothes very similar to ours (Australia, North America).

Next return to the map of the Isle of Struay and talk about it as a place that is both similar and different to the local area.

Tell the children that they are now going to look at the similarities and differences between places like Struay and the local area.

Group activities

Activity sheet 1

This sheet is aimed at children who need more support. They can draw pictures of local houses and traffic and can distinguish between these and their equivalents on Struay. They have to draw pictures of local houses, traffic and the landscape. Some children may need help with the landscape pictures, but a skyline type of view is often the best in these situations. On the back of the sheet they have to write a sentence about the two sorts of houses.

Activity sheet 2

This sheet is aimed at children who can work independently. They can readily distinguish between local types of houses, landscape, traffic and jobs. They have to draw examples from the local area and from Struay. On the back of the sheet they have to write sentences about how houses and traffic are similar and how they are different.

Activity sheet 3

This sheet is aimed at more able children. They can use words to describe houses, landscape, traffic, jobs and people both locally and on Struay. Some key words for Struay are given to help them begin the task. On the back of the sheet they have to write a comparison between Struay and the local area.

Plenary session

Share the responses to the activity sheets and talk about the similarities and differences between Struay and the local area. Add other headings to those on the activity sheets, such as 'Games we play', 'Shops we visit', 'Places we go to in our spare time' and 'Books we read'. Ask the children to draw comparisons between the local area and Struay.

Ideas for support

The children may need some support on what to draw for traffic on Struay. Talk to them about what types of traffic might be found there (refer to *Katie Morag delivers the mail*) and remind them of tractors and even bicycles. Similarly for the local landscape, you might want to suggest that the children draw a montage of local houses, flats and skyline features such as electricity pylons, cooling towers, factory chimneys or tall office blocks.

Make a collection of fruit and vegetables from around the world, concentrating on those where the country of origin is named. Give the children the fruit and vegetables and let them list the names of the countries. Then ask them to find these places on a globe or world map.

Ideas for extension

Encourage the children to look at the labels on tins of food at home and to write down the products and the countries from which they come, such as tinned tomatoes from Italy and tinned peaches from South Africa. In addition they should look at and make notes on the labels on clothes and everyday items such as footwear, computers, furniture, clocks and watches. Use the information to produce a large world map showing all the named countries and the products they have supplied to families in the class.

Ask the children to cut out all the references to other countries that they can find in a local free newspaper. This should include advertisements, such as foreign cars, local Chinese, Bengali and other foreign restaurants, goods from other countries for sale and all television programmes that relate to other countries (*Neighbours*, *Home and Away*). Ask the children to produce a wall display entitled 'The world in our town' with a world map at the centre and all the adverts around it placed on or near the country concerned.

Linked ICT activities

Talk to the children about visiting different places around the world. Show them a passport and explain what a passport is and why you need to have one to visit some countries. Using a word processing program such as 'Talking Write Away' or 'Teaxtease', create a simple template that the children have to complete with their name, age, hair colour and so on – a fact file of information about each child.

Talk to the children about what other things they might need to have on a passport that would easily identify them. They may say things like favourite food or television programme. Help them through the process by using photographs from a magazine and asking the children to describe the people in the pictures.

Take a photograph of each child, using a digital camera, and show the children how to insert the photograph onto the passport template. Print out the passport and laminate it to create a passport for the children to use. Create a role-play area in the classroom to be an airport and encourage some simple role-play activities. Try to use a computer in this area. Talk to the children about what the computer would be needed for in the airport.

Compare and contrast

Name _____

Compare and contrast

Draw a picture of Grannie's tractor in the chart below.

Draw pictures of local houses, the local landscape and local traffic in the chart below.

	Struay	Our area
Houses		
Landscape		
Traffic		

On the back of this sheet write a sentence about houses in your area and in Struay.

Name _____

Compare and contrast

Draw pictures in the chart below of traffic and jobs in Struay.

Draw pictures of local houses, landscape, traffic and jobs in the chart.

	Struay	Our area
Houses		
Landscape		
Traffic		
Jobs		

On the back of this sheet, write sentences to say how houses and traffic in your local area are similar to and different from those in Struay.

Name _____

Compare and contrast

Write words to describe the houses, landscape, traffic, jobs and people in Struay in the chart below. Some key words for Struay are given to help you.
Now do the same for your local area.

	Struay	Our area
Houses	cottages	
Landscape	mountains, islands	
Traffic	tractors	
Jobs	farming	
People	lady artist	

On the back of this sheet, write sentences comparing your local area with Struay.

Likes and dislikes

This chapter uses the island of Dominica in the Caribbean to provide additional information and ideas about likes and dislikes.

Introducing Dominica

Dominica (population 74,000) is a small Caribbean island not to be confused with the Dominican Republic (which shares the large island of Hispaniola with Haiti). Because it has very few sandy beaches and only a small airport, Dominica was largely ignored in the first wave of tourist development in the Caribbean during the 1970s. Most visitors come from the cruise ships that stop at the island for a day or so. Dominica provides a glimpse of life in a Caribbean island before the tourist invasion.

Much of the rainforest in Dominica is still intact, although clearing for banana cultivation has reduced it, especially near the coast. Banana cultivation and export is the largest source of employment and income for Dominica. The villages and towns, such as Roseau (population 21,000), have changed little in recent years and the carnival is for the benefit of local people, not tourists.

Dominica is an island where it is hot and wet nearly all year. These conditions are ideal for the growth of plants and so the rainforest on the island is thick and luxuriant. The rainforest is rich in wildlife and covers the mountains, which make up the central part of the island.

There is not much flat land on Dominica, so villages tend to cluster on the coast where fishing provides a reasonable standard of living. The warm coastal waters around Dominica are home to many different types of fish so fishing has become an important local industry.

Dominica has been largely ignored in the tourist boom of the Caribbean and because of this the local markets are still important as centres that allow local people to buy and sell goods. However, there is a plan to extend the local airport in order to accommodate bigger planes that would bring in more tourists. Many local people are in favour of this because it will bring more income to the island and its people. Other people are not keen on the idea because they see how tourism has greatly changed traditional ways of life in other Caribbean islands, such as Barbados and Trinidad.

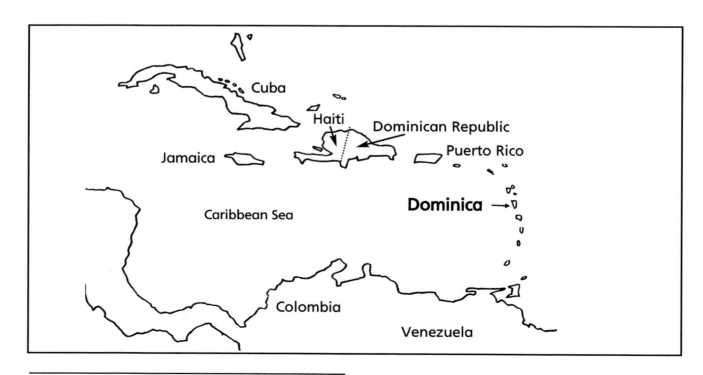

Likes and dislikes

Geography objective (Unit 3)
• To identify likes and dislikes about a place.

Resources

- Generic sheets 1–3 (pages 55–57)
- Activity sheets 1–3 (pages 58–60)
- A map of Struay from one of the *Katie Morag* stories
- A globe

Starting points: *whole class*

Tell the children that they are going to think about what things they like or dislike about different places.

Show them Generic sheet 1 on an OHP or in an enlarged version and the map of Struay. Explain that you want them to think about what it would be like to live on the Isle of Struay, especially what they would like and dislike. Ask questions such as:

- What would you do when you wanted to go to the shops?
- How would you get to the cinema?
- How do people get around on Struay?
- Are there any play areas?
- Would you like visiting the farms and seeing the animals?

Once the children have grasped some of the key advantages and disadvantages of living on Struay, start to fill in Generic sheet 1 with the things the children like and dislike about the houses, shops, play areas and so on. If there are disagreements, take a vote and record how many like or dislike the feature.

For the box labelled 'Other things' encourage the children to suggest additional things about living on Struay that they would like or dislike, such as visiting friends and relatives.

Now show them Generic sheets 2 and 3 on an OHP or in an enlarged version. Explain that this is another island, in this case the real island of Dominica in the Caribbean. Use the globe to

locate Dominica. Some of the key points to make are:

- Dominica is an island.
- It is hot and rainy.
- Thick rainforest grows on the mountains in the middle of the island.
- Most people live on the coast.

Now go through the pictures of life in Dominica on the generic sheets and bring out these key points:

- Many people fish for a living in Dominica.
- Other people grow bananas.
- People live in houses made from wood and corrugated iron.
- Bananas are packed in boxes and loaded onto boats.
- Most of the bananas come to the UK.
- Roseau is the capital and main town.
- People travel to Roseau by bus.
- On Saturdays there is a market in Roseau. People buy and sell flowers, fruit, vegetables and fish.
- Every year there is a big carnival and parade in Roseau.

Tell the children that they are now going to think about what they might like or dislike about the island of Dominica.

Group activities

Activity sheet 1
This sheet is aimed at children who need more support. They can identify at least three things they would like and three things they would dislike about Dominica. They have to draw a picture for each like and each dislike and label what they have drawn.

Activity sheet 2
This sheet is aimed at children who can work independently. They can identify a range of things that they like and dislike about Dominica. They

have to write their likes and dislikes in the boxes. On the back of the sheet they have to draw pictures of the two things they would most like about Dominica.

Activity sheet 3

This sheet is aimed at more able children. They are able to write fluently and can make an informed personal choice. They have to write a few sentences about:

- why they would or would not like to visit Dominica;
- what things they think they would like about Dominica;
- what things they think they would dislike about Dominica.

Plenary session

Share the responses to the activity sheets. Discuss what features of Dominica most of the children like and those most dislike. Talk about how similar Dominica is to Struay. Has anyone been to a different island? Was it similar to or different from either Struay or Dominica? Together, on the board draw up a chart to show the similarities and differences.

Ideas for support

Ask the children to draw pictures of features of their home that they like and dislike. These might include their bedroom, the bathroom, the sitting room and so on. Try to get them to say why they like or dislike the particular place and to write a few words to accompany the pictures.

Then ask the children to talk about places within the school that they like and dislike. These might include the playground, the classroom and the entrance hall. Then ask them to draw pictures of places they like and dislike and use these as a wall display on 'Places in school we like', and 'Places in school we dislike'.

Ideas for extension

Encourage the children to find more information about life in Dominica. They could use holiday brochures that you have obtained from travel agents, books or CD-Roms (especially for information on weather and bananas). You could also encourage the children to write to the Dominican High Commission in London. Use all the data collected to make a wall display of life in Dominica.

Ask the children to draw a sequence of pictures to show how bananas get from the trees in Dominica to small boats, then to ships which travel to the UK, then to lorries which take them to UK supermarkets and markets.

Ask the children to look at pictures of other places. These could be other places in the local area, such as the leisure centre, the library, the park or the shopping centre. Ask the children to say why they like some of these places and why they dislike others. Ask them to draw pictures to illustrate each of the places, and to write suggestions of how places they dislike could be improved (more green spaces, more litter bins, more seats).

The same idea of places that children like or dislike can be developed in relation to more distant places. Use photos from travel brochures to illustrate some of the features of distant places. These will naturally tend to be images of things children will like (such as the sea or sandy beaches), but ask the children to think about other things not shown on the photos, such as rubbish tips or industrial areas.

Linked ICT activities

Tell the children that they are going to create a picture for a T-shirt to wear on holiday to Dominica. Talk to them about the different things they have found out about Dominica. Talk about the weather and the different types of food. Encourage them to think about the types of images or symbols they would want to put on a T-shirt to advertise Dominica, such as sunshine or bananas. Using a graphics program such as 'Dazzle', 'Granada Colours' or 'Fresco', show the children how to use the draw, shape and fill tools to create their logo. Print out the completed logos.

From a sheet of A4 paper cut out the shape of a T-shirt and display the logo in the centre of the T-shirt. These can then be added to a wall display on Dominica. Alternatively, pin a line of string across the classroom and display them clipped to the line. They can look really effective if the T-shirts are all different colours.

Likes and dislikes

	Things I like	Things I dislike
Houses		
Shops		
Weather		
Places to play		
Places for entertainment		
Getting around		
Other things		

Dominica

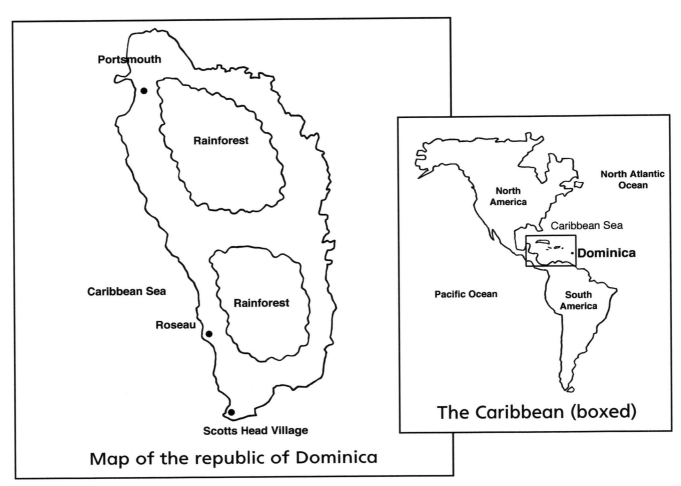

Map of the republic of Dominica

The Caribbean (boxed)

Fishermen gathering sprats

The main shopping street in Roseau

Dominica

Bus

Bananas on a tree

House of wood and corrugated iron

Boats and a ship

Name _____

Likes and dislikes

Draw three things you think you would like about Dominica.
Label your pictures.
Draw and label three things you think you would dislike about Dominica.

What I would like about Dominica	What I would dislike about Dominica
1	1
2	2
3	3

Name _____

Likes and dislikes

Write in the boxes the things you think you would like or dislike about the island of Dominica.

	Like	Dislike
Houses		
Shops		
Weather		
Places to play		
Places for entertainment		
Getting around		
Other things		

On the back of this sheet, draw pictures of the two things you think you would like most about Dominica.

Name _____

Likes and dislikes

I think I would/would not like to visit Dominica because:

I think the things I would like about Dominica are:

I think the things I would dislike about Dominica are:

Places we have visited

CHAPTER 7

TEACHERS' NOTES

The focus of this chapter is to help children locate places that they have visited. These places can be located on maps of the UK, maps of Europe and globes. However, it is important that children are introduced to these maps in a considered way.

Developing map and atlas skills

Chapter 1 provides help to introduce children to the different elements of maps, such as signs and symbols, plan view, direction, distance and location.

Potentially, atlas maps and globes can be difficult for children, but here are some guidelines to help:

- Start with a globe. Stress that the world is three-dimensional. The bigger the globe, the better – and there are now some excellent inflatable globes.

- Get the children to find their country on the globe and then ask them to find neighbouring countries, such as the Republic of Ireland, as well as France, Spain and Belgium.

- Then go to an atlas map of the UK. Relate the countries of the UK seen on the globe to the same countries shown on the atlas map. Try to find some of the main cities on both globe and atlas, such as London, Edinburgh and Cardiff.

- Use atlas maps as often as you can with the children. The more you use them, the more familiar and less confusing they will be to the children. Use overhead transparencies of some atlas pages and point to particular places such as rivers, cities or seaside places so that you are certain that the children are looking at the correct part of the map.

- If in doubt, **keep it simple**. Don't worry about scale, projections or the minute detail shown on many atlas maps. Keep to named countries, towns and rivers and a few seas and oceans.

Because atlases contain so much information, try to focus on a small part of a map at a time. For example, find a map of the south coast of England and identify which areas are sea and which are land. Name the English Channel. Talk about some of the main towns shown on the map, such as Dover and Folkestone and make sure the children can locate these on their copy of the atlas.

Ask the children to point out features shown on the map, such as the main roads (usually shown in red) and motorways (usually shown in blue). Ask them to try and locate railway lines (usually shown in black). In each case ask the children to check with the key to ensure which colours do relate to which features. Towns are often shown in red or orange. Try to get the children to spot physical features such as the rivers, which are usually shown in blue. Other features such as lakes and estuaries, also stand out well on maps of the UK. If the map uses colour to show the height of the land, ask the children to find the names of some of the areas of higher land shown, such as the Downs (North or South) or the Weald, or hills such as the Chilterns and the Cotswolds. In these ways you will help children to begin to make sense of the maps used in atlases.

Places we have visited

Geography objectives (Unit 4)
- To name and investigate places.
- To use geographical terms.
- To use maps and atlases.

Resources

- Generic sheets 1 and 2 (pages 64 and 65)
- Activity sheets 1–3 (pages 66–68)
- Large maps of the UK, Europe and the world
- A marker pen

Starting points: *whole class*

Tell the children that they are going to think about places they have visited. Some visits may have been holidays, some may have been to see relatives. Ask questions such as:

- What are some of the places you have visited lately?
- Where is it? (seaside, town, country, in the UK, in Europe)

For each answer, ask:

- What is it like?

As the children answer, locate each place on the appropriate map (of the UK, Europe, the world) and then mark and name the places on Generic sheets 1 or 2 on an OHP or on an enlarged version, or on a blank world map. Try to get a balance between places visited in the UK and places visited abroad. Ask questions such as:

- What did you do when you were there?
- What was the weather like?
- What were the local people like?

As the opportunities present themselves, ask the children to label England, Wales, Scotland, Northern Ireland and, if possible, some of the closest European countries such as the Republic of Ireland, France, Belgium, Spain and Portugal. On the map of the UK, they could mark the following places with a red dot and label them: London, Birmingham, Newcastle, Belfast, Swansea, Edinburgh, Cardiff, Glasgow, Manchester, Sheffield,

Leeds, Southampton, Bristol and Liverpool. Again, if possible, they could label the USA and Canada on the world map.

As the list of places visited builds up, tell the children that you are going to sort the places into groups. Ask them to suggest groups. Now sort the responses into town, countryside and seaside (put seaside towns into the seaside group). Ask the children to give each group a title.

Tell the children that they are now going to study one of the places they visited.

Group activities

Activity sheet 1
This sheet is aimed at children who need more support. They are able to remember the key features of a place they have visited. They have to draw a picture, name the place and locate it (for example, Scarborough in the UK) and say if it is in a town, in the country or at the seaside. Then they have to draw a picture of what they did while they were there. On the back of the sheet, they have to draw a picture of the journey home including the type of transport.

Activity sheet 2
This sheet is aimed at children who can work independently. They are able to describe, in words and pictures, a sequence of events relating to a place they have visited and say if it is a town, in the country or at the seaside. They have to draw pictures showing them leaving home, travelling to the place, what the place was like and what they did there. In each case, they have to complete a sentence to identify the place, method of transport and activities undertaken.

Activity sheet 3
This sheet is aimed at more able children. They are very familiar with the events of a journey. They have to fill in the details of where they went, what the place was like and what they did, then finish

the story of their visit in any way they choose (for example; the return journey, something exciting that happened, who went and who they met). They should say if the place is a town, in the country or at the seaside. They add pictures to support their text.

Plenary session

Share the responses to the activity sheets. Talk about the types of transport used to visit each place and about the range of activities that the children did while they were on the visit. Ask the children if they would like to return to these places and where else they would like to go. Talk about what kinds of places they were and the similarities and differences between them.

Ideas for support

Collect a series of postcards of places in the UK, such as London, Birmingham, the Yorkshire Dales, Snowdon, the Scottish Highlands and the Cotswolds. Give these to the children for them to locate the places in the UK and name them and mark them on a map. For children who are not sure where to find the UK on a map, refer to Generic sheet 2 and an atlas map of the UK. Talk to them about where they live and locate this on the atlas map and Generic sheet 1. Then find on the maps some of the places shown on the postcards. A similar activity would use holiday brochures to identify the names of resorts, and find them on a map. It may be best at this stage to stick to places in Europe.

Any children who hesitate over places they have visited recently can be encouraged by talking about Barnaby Bear and his travels. You can say that recently Barnaby has visited places such as London (the Tower and Buckingham Palace) and the seaside at Blackpool (or similar) or other places local to your area.

Use holiday brochures to ask the children what things they would expect to do on a visit to a place (swimming, paddling, building sandcastles, theme park rides and so on).

Use large plans of the local area. Again, ask the children to identify places they have visited and then ask them to mark and name these on the large map. This can form the basis for a wall display called 'Local places we have visited'.

Ideas for extension

Give the children some brochures for holidays in faraway places. Ask them to locate these places on a world map and then plan a round-the-world trip to visit as many of these places as possible. The degree of difficulty can be varied to include calculating distances travelled and time of travel, as well as listing the range of things to do and see in each place. Give the children some material downloaded from the internet so they can check on prices and schedules for round-the-world trips, including a list of places to be visited.

Linked ICT activities

Talk to the children about the different places they have visited and been to on holiday. Tell them that they are going to let their friends know what they did on their holiday. Ask them how they would usually do that when they are on holiday. Most will say that they would send a postcard; others may say email, phone or text. Say that this time they are going to record what they did on their holiday on a tape recorder. Give them the opportunity to record their experiences in groups of two or three. Give them a time limit. It is very useful to have a classroom assistant to help with this activity.

Note: some children may not want to do this but be quite happy just talking to the class about it.

When the tapes have been completed they could be used for a listening activity or a starting point for a literacy activity.

Places we have visited

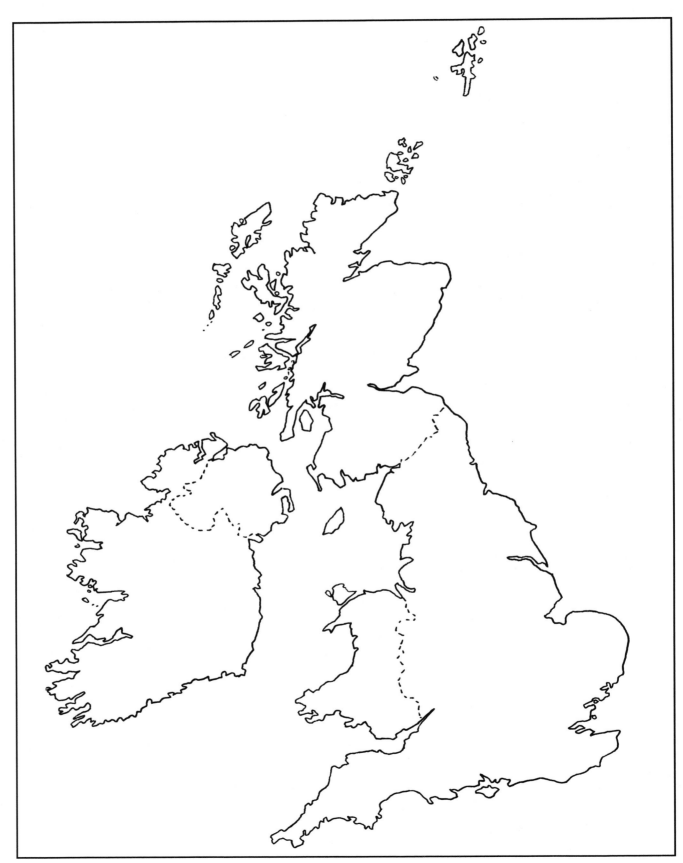

Places we have visited

Name _____

Places we have visited

Think of a place you have visited. Write its name and which country it is in. Draw a picture of the place.

Where I went: _____

Where the place is: _____

This place is a town ☐ in the countryside ☐ at the seaside ☐

Draw a picture of what you did there.

This is what I did there:

On the back of this sheet, draw a picture of your journey home, showing what transport you used.

Name _____

Places we have visited

Think of a place you have visited. Draw a picture in each box below. Complete the sentences to describe each picture. Say whether it was a town, in the countryside or at the seaside.

One sunny day I got up and went

to _____

_____

_____

We travelled on _____

_____

_____

The place was great. There were

_____

_____

_____

When I was there I _____

_____

_____

_____

Name _____

Places we have visited

Complete the sentences below.
Draw pictures in the boxes to go with them.
Finish the story of your visit in the last box.

After breakfast we left home and travelled to	This is what the place was like. You can see
This is what we did while we were there. We	

Seaside weather

CHAPTER 8

TEACHERS' NOTES

Why weather at the seaside is so important

People go to the seaside for a change of scenery and to enjoy some 'fresh air', that is unpolluted air. Seaside places have a reputation for clean unpolluted air and this is largely based on the breezes that blow regularly between the land and the sea. The normal pattern during the summer in the UK is that during the morning there is a breeze from the land to the sea and during the afternoon, as the land heats up, the breeze is reversed and blows from the cooler sea to the land.

In the same way, this pattern of land and sea breezes is the basis for much of the attraction of sailing in coastal areas. Many people who visit the seaside take a trip in a boat and in the past this was often a sailing vessel. These days yachts of all shapes and sizes are very popular and this is based in part on the weather conditions to be found on coasts.

However, seaside places have other attractions for both residents and visitors. Normally seaside places are milder in winter than places inland. This is because the sea acts as a moderating influence, keeping the temperatures a little higher in the winter and so avoiding some of the frosts and snow that may be common inland.

In some seaside places, storms can be a problem. This is especially true on hot summer days. Then the air over the land gets very hot and is close to much cooler air over the sea. When the hot and cool air come into conflict, thunderstorms, with high winds, rain and even hail, can be quite common.

Weather, people and places

Weather is something that children experience directly every day. They can all contribute information on the effects weather has on the pattern of their daily lives, such as school closures in snowy weather.

Some key activities to reinforce the link between weather and people and places are listed below:

- Undertake a close study of the sky to observe the changing colours and cloud shapes throughout the day.

- Make simple daily records of the weather and its changes.

- Link changes in weather to changes in clothing, food, activities, buildings (such as the need for steeply sloping roofs to remove rain and snow from houses) and wildlife (such as the problems of finding food in winter).

- Study the television weather forecasts to get used to the patterns of weather around the UK and discuss the accuracy of the forecasts.

- Make a collection of weather sayings, such as 'Red sky at night, shepherd's delight' and discuss what they mean and how true they are.

- Local weather centres, Ceefax, television and online weather centres provide a wealth of information for particular localities around the country. This is especially important in relation to localised weather, such as fog, ice and high winds, and is particularly relevant to activities such as hill walking, windsurfing and potholing.

- Identify with the children the different elements that make up weather – cloud, wind, rain, sun and how warm it is (temperature).

- Cut out a series of pictures from magazines and catalogues for the children to sort into sets related to different types of weather, such as hot, cold, wet and dry.

- Give the children fabrics to test – samples of clothing for different purposes. The aim is to test the fabrics for properties related to weather conditions, such as elasticity, water repellency, insulation and rot resistance.

- Show and discuss pictures of weather vanes, such as arrows, cockerels or ships, and then ask the children to design and make their own. Remind the children of the points of the compass (perhaps paint them on the playground). Stress the importance of remembering that winds are named according to the direction from which they come: a north wind blows from the north.

- A simple instrument to measure the strength of the wind can easily be designed and made by groups of children (see diagrams below) and the varying wind strengths can be recorded on a graph.

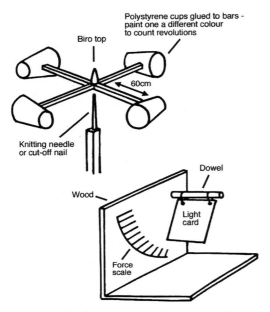

wind-measuring instruments

- Investigate the patterns on windows, branches and fences on frosty days. These patterns can be drawn and then the children can investigate other questions, such as:

  – How does frost change when the sun comes out?
  – What do you notice about your breath on frosty days?
  – Listen carefully to your footsteps on frosty grass. How is it different from walking on unfrosty grass?

- Illustrate the following with a series of pictures:

  the story of a thunderstorm from a small, dark cloud, through its build-up into massive clouds, together with the thunder, lightning

and torrential rain, leading to a final clear-up.

The pictures can then be sequenced to tell the story of one thunderstorm.

- Pictures of homes in different countries can be used to illustrate the impact of weather on how people live, such as the tents used by people who live in the desert; white, flat-roofed houses in hot, dry places to reflect the heat and for use as storage areas; and steep-roofed houses in wet, tropical areas to get rid of the rain.

- On snowy days, children could fill ten empty yoghurt pots with fresh snow (not packed down). When this is left to melt indoors the children can see how much snow would be needed to fill one yoghurt pot (ten pots are about the average).

- On a wet day, ask the children to study where the rain collects in puddles. Ask them to try to explain why puddles form in particular places and not in others (answers could include the slope of the ground or a dip in the surface). Also ask the children to notice the surface on which puddles form (mostly on tarmac and concrete, not grass).

- Get the children to draw round some of the puddles in the playground using chalk. Then ask them to compare and draw the different shapes of the puddles. As the puddles dry out, ask the children to go back and draw round each puddle again. Ask questions such as:

  – Which puddles seem to shrink the fastest?
  – Why is this? (Usually the shallower the puddle and the greater its surface area, the faster it will evaporate.)

- On a windy day, ask the children to look out of the classroom window. Ask them to identify the clues which show that it is a windy day (trees bending, branches moving, leaves being blown off or blown about). Then get the children to draw a picture to incorporate all the clues they have identified to show that it is a windy day.

Seaside weather

Geography objectives (Unit 4)
- To investigate a place.
- To learn about the effects of weather on people and their surroundings.

Resources
- Generic sheets 1 and 2 (pages 73 and 74)
- Activity sheets 1–3 (pages 75–77)
- A map of the UK
- A marker pen

Starting points: *whole class*

Tell the children that they are going to look at seaside places and seaside weather. Ask questions such as:

- Who has been to the seaside?
- Where did you go?
- When did you go?
- What did you do while you were there?

Identify the nearest seaside place to the school on a map of the UK.

Then locate Blackpool on the map. Show the children the picture of Blackpool on Generic sheet 1 on an OHP or in an enlarged version. Encourage them to identify the key features of Blackpool and, as they do, to write each one on the picture:

- the tower
- hotels
- the pier
- the funfair
- the beach
- icecream stalls
- the sea
- boats.

Next, talk about all the different things that children can do in a seaside place like Blackpool:

- swim
- paddle
- go up the tower
- go on the funfair rides
- play beach games such as cricket, football, tennis
- sail model boats or go on real ones
- relax
- eat fish and chips.

Now, still looking at Generic sheet 1, ask the children how the scene would look different in winter:

- very few people
- stalls closed
- no one on the beach
- no one in the sea
- no boats.

Now show the children Generic sheet 2 on an OHP or in an enlarged version, and explain that it shows a series of weather symbols and the weather for five days. Talk about each symbol with the children and then ask:

- What was the weather like on Monday afternoon? (windy)
- What was the weather like on Tuesday morning? (sunny)
- What was the weather like on Wednesday? (cloudy)
- When did it rain? (Tuesday afternoon, Friday morning)
- How many times was it windy? (four)

Explain to the children that the scene in Blackpool varies a lot with the weather. In summer, if it is sunny, it is a busy place. In winter, if it is cold and wet, it is very quiet. Tell them that they are now going to look at how the weather affects lots of things in our lives, from the clothes we wear to the games we play.

Group activities

Activity sheet 1
This sheet is aimed at children who need more support. They can recognise different types of

clothing and how this relates to the weather. They have to colour in the items for Amy's holiday in a hot place. On the back of the sheet they have to draw a picture of Amy playing at the seaside.

Activity sheet 2

This sheet is aimed at children who can work independently. They can use weather symbols to describe the weather and relate this to the most appropriate types of clothing. They have to colour in the clothes that Amy needs for five days. On the back of the sheet they have to draw pictures of two things Amy might do in the snow and write two sentences to describe the pictures.

Activity sheet 3

This sheet is aimed at more able children. They can understand weather symbols and can decide whether activities are affected by the weather. They have to describe the weather in five days in January and five days in July. Then they have to group a range of games and sports according to whether they are winter, summer or all-year activities.

Plenary session

Share the responses to the activity sheets. Talk about the different ways in which the weather affects the things people wear and the games they play. Ask questions such as:

- How does the weather affect what we eat? (Hot soup in winter and cold drinks in summer.)
- How does the weather affect where we eat? (Picnics and barbecues in a UK summer often get rained off.)

Talk about Generic sheet 1. Ask questions such as 'What do people do in Blackpool on sunny days?' Then ask 'What do people do in Blackpool on rainy days?' (Think of indoor amusement arcades.)

Ideas for support

Get the children to record the weather each day for a week, each morning and each afternoon, using the symbols on Generic sheet 2 (see page 74). Ask them to devise other symbols for different types of weather, such as fog or gales. Use the symbols as part of a display with the title 'Today's weather is' and let the children pin up the symbols twice each day.

Encourage the children to think about how weather can be dangerous (for example, high winds bring down trees which block roads, heavy rain floods houses, seaside storms damage boats, fog causes motorway pile-ups). Then ask them to draw pictures illustrating some of the ways in which weather can create danger.

Ideas for extension

Encourage the children to think about how the weather changes over the course of a year. Ask them to draw four pictures to illustrate the types of weather, clothes and events typical of January (snow, ice, thick clothes), April (spring flowers, lambs), July (building sandcastles on the beach) and October (leaves falling from trees). Then relate the different weather to the seasons and talk about winter, spring, summer and autumn.

Ask the children to draw a picture of a scene on a windy day. Tell them to make it very clear which way the wind is blowing (clothes on a line, smoke from a chimney, kite flying, leaves being blown from a tree, people leaning into the wind).

Linked ICT activities

Give the children some pictures from a magazine or holiday brochure or some holiday photographs, all showing different types of weather. Talk to them about the pictures and what the weather is like in each one. Ask them to look for other clues in the pictures that tell us what the weather is like, such as the clothes people are wearing. Look at the backgrounds of the pictures – the sky, the sea and the fields – what can they tell us about the types of weather in the pictures?

Tell the children that they are going to create their own picture of a holiday scene. They must first decide on what the weather is going to be like in the picture and what they will need to add to it for it to appear either a summer or a winter holiday. Using a graphics program such as 'Dazzle', 'Fresco' or 'Granada Colours', show them how to create the background of the image first, by adding the sky and fields, mountains or a beach using the draw and fill tool. They should save the background and then add the images in the foreground that will show what is happening in the picture. The children could add some clip art to the picture.

Seaside weather

Weather symbols

Day	Morning	Afternoon
Monday	☀ sunny	🚩 windy
Tuesday	☀ sunny	☔ rainy
Wednesday	☁ cloudy	☁ cloudy
Thursday	☀ / 🚩 sunny / windy	☀ sunny
Friday	☔ rainy	🚩 windy

Key
☀ sunny
☁ cloudy
☔ rainy
🚩 windy

Name _____

Seaside weather

Amy is going on holiday to a hot place. She is packing her suitcase.
Colour in red all the things she needs to take with her.

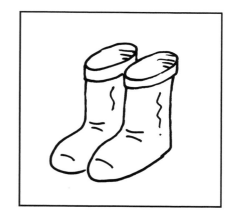

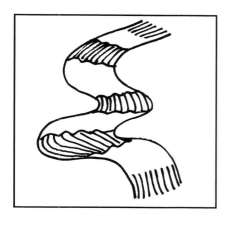

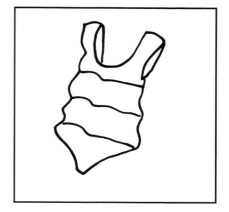

On the back of this sheet, draw a picture of Amy playing at the seaside.

Name _____

Seaside weather

This is Amy's weather chart. It shows five days in January.
Colour in red the clothes she should wear for these five days.

Monday	Tuesday	Wednesday	Thursday	Friday
snow	snow	sun and frost	snow	cloud

On the back of this sheet, draw two things Amy might do in the snow.
Write a sentence about each thing that Amy is doing.

_____

Name _____

Seaside weather

These charts show the weather in January (top) and July (below). In the spaces write words to describe the weather each day.

Monday	Tuesday	Wednesday	Thursday	Friday

Monday	Tuesday	Wednesday	Thursday	Friday

Below is a list of sports and games. Some are played mostly in summer, some in winter and some can be played all year. Write the name of each sport in the correct column.

cricket   sledging   snowballing   football   swimming
skating   rugby   table tennis   squash   tennis

Sports and games played mostly in winter	Sports and games played mostly in summer	Sports and games played all year round

Seaside and home

This chapter uses aerial photos and letter/number grids as a means of comparing localities.

Using aerial photos

There are now many sources of high quality aerial photos (such as Geonex UK, Barwell Business Park, Arthur Street, Barwell, Leicestershire LE9 8GZ Tel: 01455 844513), so children can quickly become used to seeing views from above. An aerial view of your school and its immediate surroundings is an excellent starting point. At this stage, it is better to concentrate on oblique aerial photos rather than the more difficult vertical aerial photos, which show the view from directly above. Oblique pictures make it easier to recognise places and objects. Ask the children to locate the school and its car park, and then ask them to locate a series of streets and features close to the school. Remind them that these features will probably look different because they are seen from above.

Try to combine using the aerial photos with a study of a map or A–Z plan of the area around the school. Keep it simple but encourage the children to identify places such as road junctions, parks, lakes and large buildings on both the aerial photo and the map or plan. Talk about how we can recognise features from the air by their shapes.

Seaside places are good sites for the use of aerial photos because there is usually a distinct line separating the land from the sea. Key features such as castles, towers, bays and beaches also show up clearly on aerial photos. Try putting tracing paper or acetate over the aerial photos and asking the children to write in the names of the key features – for example, cliffs, pier, beach and sand dunes.

Seaside and home

Geography objectives (Unit 4)
- To use aerial photographs (and aerial views).
- To compare their own locality with a different locality (seaside).

Resources

- Generic sheets 1–3 (pages 81–83)
- Activity sheets 1–3 (pages 84–86)
- A map of the UK
- An aerial photograph of the school
- A marker pen

Starting points: *whole class*

Tell the children that they are going to look at the seaside town of Scarborough. Locate Scarborough on a map of the UK. Ask questions such as:

- What are the names of some of the nearby towns and cities? (Whitby, Bridlington, York)
- What is the name of the sea? (North Sea)

Show the children the aerial drawing of Scarborough on Generic sheet 1 on an OHP or in an enlarged version. Explain that this is an aerial view of the seaside town from above and looking down on Scarborough. Ask the children to identify some of the key features shown by the arrows. These should include:

- the castle
- the harbour
- the beach
- the road
- the sea
- boats in the harbour
- houses
- hotels.

As each point is identified, label it.

Then use three headings on the OHP or board:

- Things found in our area but not in Scarborough.
- Things found in Scarborough but not in our area.
- Things found in both our area and Scarborough.

Ask the children what things would be found only in Scarborough (harbour, pier, ships, beach, sea, castle). As each one is identified, add it to the correct column. Next ask what things are found only in our area (factories, office blocks, motorways). Write these in the correct column. Then ask what things are found in both our area and Scarborough (houses, hotels, shops, pubs, restaurants, main roads).

Now show the children Generic sheet 2 on an OHP or in an enlarged version. Explain that this is a map of the same part of Scarborough as the aerial view. Ask questions such as:

- What are the names of the two parts of the harbour? (Old and East)
- What is the name of the road behind the beach? (Foreshore Road)

Next show the children Generic sheet 3 on an OHP or in an enlarged version. Use the top picture to talk about addresses. In the bookcase what is the address of the ball? Tell the children they need to look along the bottom of the bookcase to the letter C first and then up the side to the number 3. So the ball's address is C3. Now ask them to give you the addresses of the other items in the bookcase.

Next show the children the grid at the bottom of the sheet. Talk about the address for the hat being A3. Say that when we use maps we don't really talk about addresses but use references, so A3 is the reference. Then ask them for the references for the other things in the grid.

Now refer back to the grid on Generic sheet 2. Explain that it is there to help us find places. So, for example, Sandside is in square D5. Stress the importance of giving the letter along the bottom of the map first and the number from the side of the map second. This is vital for what comes later when four-figure grid references are used. Ask questions such as:

- In which square is the Old Harbour? (D5)
- In which square is the castle? (D6)

Tell the children that they are now going to look at a map with a grid to see how it can be used to find people and places.

Group activities

Activity sheet 1
This sheet is aimed at children who need more support. They are able to use the basic letter/number grid to locate places. They have to give the references of grid squares for a number of objects. Then they have to identify what objects are to be found at particular grid squares.

Activity sheet 2
This sheet is aimed at children who can work independently. They are more familiar with using letter/number grids to locate people and places. They have to use the grid to give the references for children in a classroom. Then they have to identify children at particular grid references.

Activity sheet 3
This sheet is aimed at more able children. They are very familiar with letter/number grids. They have to give the references of squares for particular sports activities and identify what can be found in other grid squares. Then they have to follow grid reference directions around the map.

Plenary session

Share the responses to the activity sheets. Talk about the use of letter/number grids to locate places and stress the importance of giving the letter before the number. If there is time, revise some of the key features of the Scarborough map, using the grid; for example, ask for the name of a road in square C5 (Eastborough, Long Westgate) or ask which squares Marine Drive is in (D7, D6, E6, E5, D5).

Ask the children to talk about features of Scarborough that are the same as in their home area (houses, shops) and those that are not found in the local area (headlands, beaches, harbour, castle) unless they live in a similar area.

Ideas for support

Give the children a grid similar to that on Activity sheet 1, but with no objects in it and no reference letters or numbers. Explain to the children how to label each grid square – for example, A1, A2, A3, then B1, B2, B3 and so on. Then tell the children to continue labelling each square on the grid.

Give the children a blank grid and ask them to draw a pirate island on it including swamps, cliffs, caves and buried treasure. Ask them to give the reference of the square in which the treasure is buried.

Ideas for extension

Ask the children to draw a detailed treasure map on an 8 by 8 grid (labelled A to H and 1 to 8). It should have a wide range of features – mountains, forests, shark-infested bays, wrecked ships, sandbanks and coral reefs. They should not mark the treasure itself. Ask them to write an old-looking letter to go with the map, describing how to reach the buried treasure. It might start with 'I staggered ashore (E5), half drowned but with the treasure safe. I set off inland through Deadman's Swamp (C4 and D3)…'

Linked ICT activities

Make a grid on the floor using masking tape or something similar which can easily be removed without causing any damage to the floor. Mark out a simple grid similar to that on Generic sheet 3. Make each square about the size of an A4 sheet of paper. Tell the children that they are going to use the Roamer (or some other remote-controlled vehicle) to move around the grid. Put some seaside objects – a shell, a bucket, a spade – into some of the squares.

Show the children how to make the Roamer move forwards and backwards and turn left and right. Let them work in small groups of four or five. Give each child a grid reference to move the Roamer to. Work with the children to move the Roamer around the grid, collecting all the objects that have been left in each of the different sections.

(If you are using the Roamer, remember that moving it forward one unit is about the same length as a sheet of A4 paper).

Scarborough

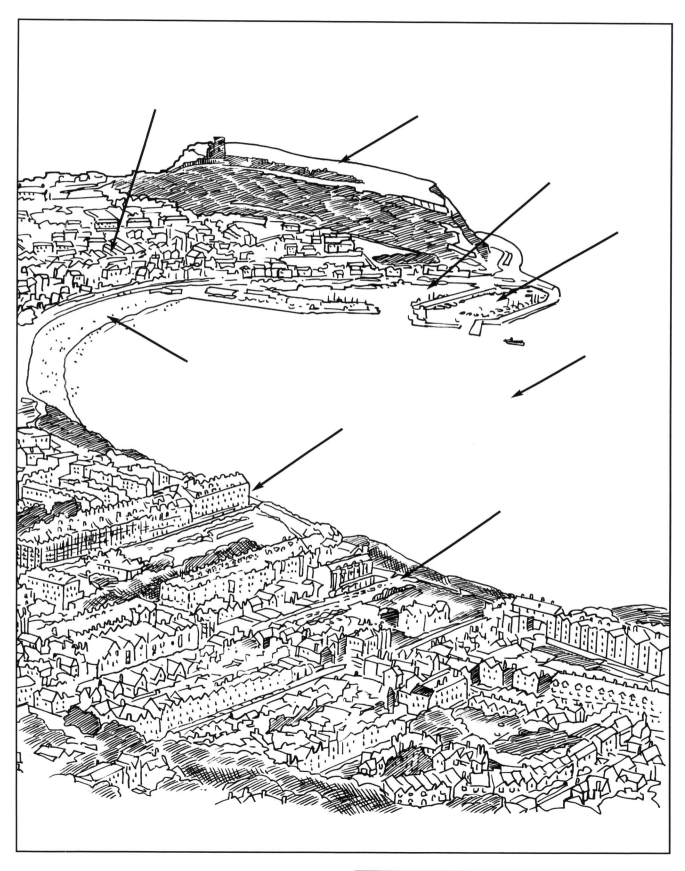

Scarborough map

GENERIC SHEET 2

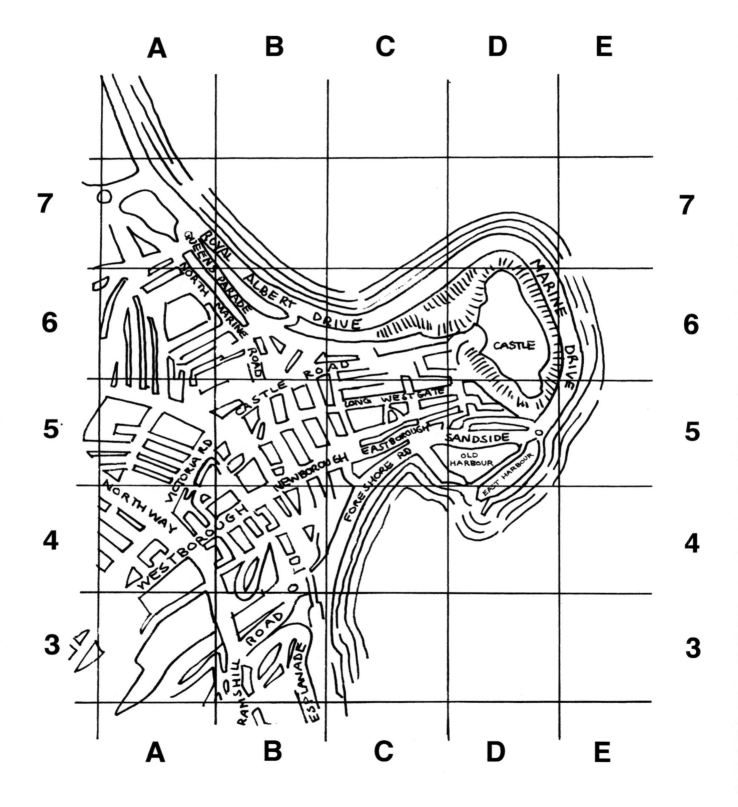

Seaside and home

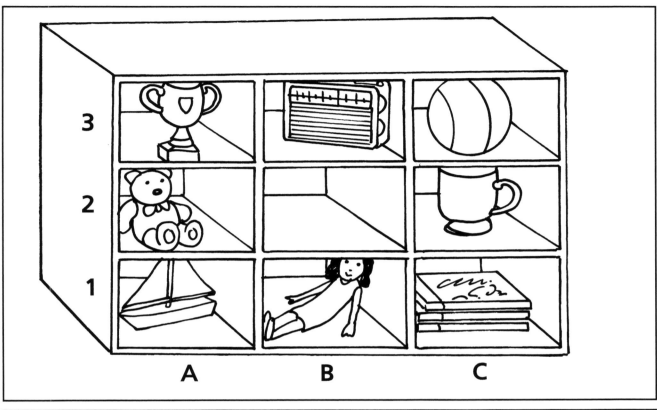

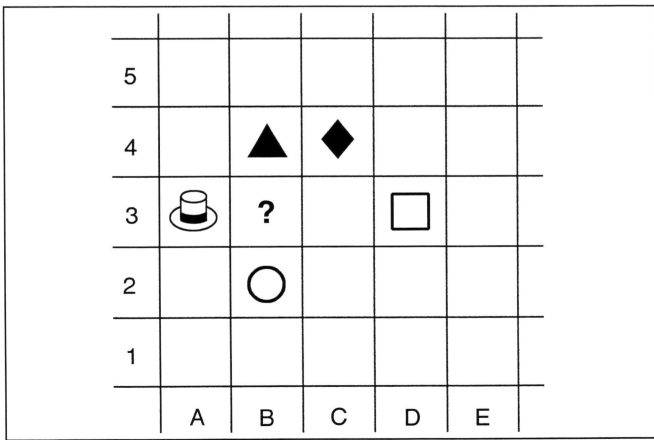

Name _____

Seaside and home

Look at the grid. The knife is in square B3.
Write the grid square references for:

- the flower _____
- the plate _____
- the violin _____

- the mug _____
- the guitar _____
- the watch _____

What do you find at these grid squares?

- B5 _____   • C3 _____   • D3 _____

- D1 _____   • A4 _____

Name _____

Seaside and home

This map shows a classroom. The teacher is in grid square E6.
Write the grid square references for:

- Amy _____
- Michael _____
- Ursula _____

- Ali _____
- Ravi _____

Which children are in these squares?

- A2 _____
- C1 _____
- D3 _____

- A5 _____
- F2 _____

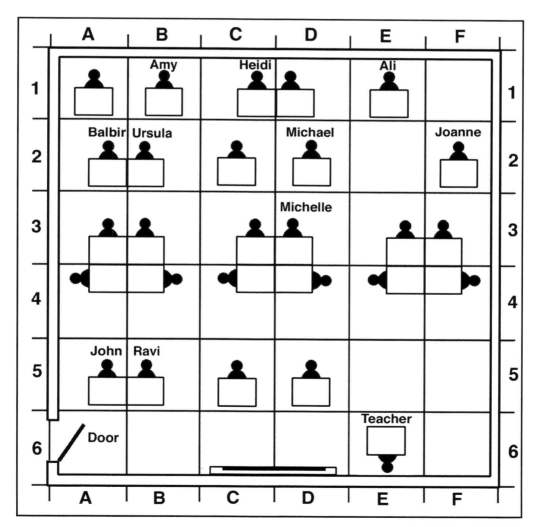

Which square is the door in? _____

Which squares is the board in? _____

Seaside and home

This is a map of a leisure centre. Write the grid square references for:
- the exercisers
- the showers
- reception

What are in these grid squares:
- B6?
- E7?
- G2?
- A5?
- A2?

Start in grid square H4. Go 7 squares west. Where are you?
Now go 1 square south. Where are you?
Now go 5 squares east. Where are you?

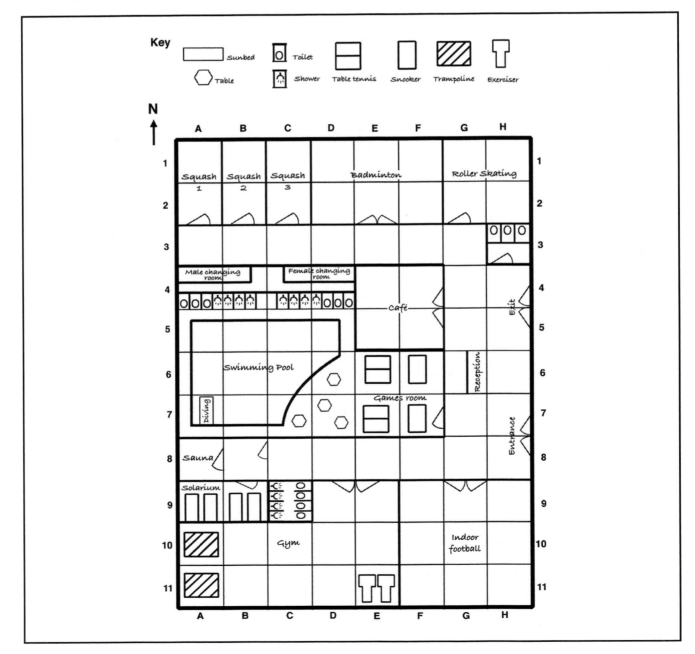

Past and present

CHAPTER 10

TEACHERS' NOTES

Comparisons between past and present

One of the best ways to focus on comparisons between the seaside in the past and the seaside today is to have a list of topics for comparison similar to the one below, which compares today with the early 1900s. This will help discussion about the similarities and differences between the two.

Seaside places, and particularly holiday resorts such as Southport, are not new. The Romans used Bath as a holiday resort.

	Seaside past	**Seaside present**
Clothes	Very smart clothes. Very different bathing clothes. Men wore straw hats.	Very casual clothes. Bikinis.
Transport	Travel to the resort by train. A few rich people travelled to the resort by car.	Most people travel to the resort by car, a few by train.
The beach	Very formal games. Children had to sit and be quiet. Donkey rides.	Games of football and cricket. Punch and Judy.
The place	People used to like to walk out over the sea so piers were very popular.	Piers now have lots of amusements and entertainments.
Where to stay	Hotels and boarding houses.	Still hotels and boarding houses but now more self-catering flats, caravans, etc.

In the eighteenth century it became fashionable for the richer members of society to 'take the waters' at spas like Brighton and Harrogate.

Later, in the nineteenth century, the new railways allowed many more people to visit the seaside and thousands of people flocked from big cities like Manchester, Glasgow and London to coastal resorts. Southport, Ayr, Clacton and Rhyl are all good examples of places that grew rapidly at this time.

Even in the 1950s, most people in the UK had only one or two weeks of paid holiday each year, and they spent them at coastal resorts such as Scarborough and Blackpool. The idea of clean, unpolluted air and a relaxed, semi-rural way of life persuaded many people in later life to retire to places like Southport.

Southport as a resort
Southport is a classic example of a coastal resort, with its sands and its seafront. Over the years the attractions of Southport have been developed by the town council to include parks, swimming pools and a pier. Victorian and Edwardian visitors were obsessed with the idea of 'walking out' on a pier above the waves so that they could look down on the sea and marine life.

LESSON PLAN

Past and present

Geography objectives (Unit 4)
• To identify features of the seaside in the past.
• To make comparisons with the seaside today.

Resources

• Generic sheets 1 and 2 (pages 90 and 91)
• Activity sheets 1–3 (pages 92–94)
• A large map of the UK

Starting points: *whole class*

Tell the children that they are going to look at what seaside places were like in the past and how they compare with today. Show them the top picture on Generic sheet 1 on an OHP or in an enlarged version, and tell them that it shows the beach at Southport in the 1890s. Show the children the location of Southport on the map of the UK and identify the cities of Manchester, Preston and Liverpool.

Ask the children questions about the first picture, such as:

• Are there many people?
• What sort of clothes are they wearing?
• What are the hats like?
• What games can you see children playing?
• What else is there for children to do?

Next ask the children to look at the second picture on Generic sheet 1. Explain that this shows people leaving Manchester for a day out in Southport in the 1890s. Ask questions such as:

• Would it be like that today?
• How would most people get to Southport today?

Now show the children Generic sheet 2 on an OHP or in an enlarged version. Explain that these are pictures of Southport in the 1890s. One shows the pier that people used to visit and the other shows one of the trams that people used for getting about the town. Ask questions such as:

• How would people travel around in Southport now?

• What sort of entertainments and shops would you expect to find on the pier?

Tell the children that they are now going to compare Southport today to how it was in the past.

Group activities

Activity sheet 1
This sheet is aimed at children who need more support. Alongside labelled pictures from the 1890s, they have to draw pictures to show present-day clothing, bathing, transport and beach activities.

Activity sheet 2
This sheet is aimed at children who can work independently. They are able to relate objects and activities in the past to their modern equivalents. They have to draw pictures of the modern-day equivalents of seaside scenes and label each picture to bring out the main contrasts.

Activity sheet 3
This sheet is aimed at more able children. They are able to write brief descriptions of pictures, given headings. They have to write descriptions of the 1890s' Victorian seaside under the headings: clothes, transport, getting around, the beach and other things they can remember, using Generic sheets 1 and 2 to help them. On the back of the sheet, they have to use the same headings to describe the modern seaside.

Plenary session

Share the responses to the activity sheets. Talk about things that have changed (getting to the seaside, clothes) and things that have not changed (donkey rides, sandcastles). Ask the children to think how Southport might look 100 years from now, using the headings: clothes, transport and the beach.

Ideas for support

Find copies of Victorian and Edwardian photographs of people at the seaside (many are available from the central public libraries in seaside places). Ask the children to study these and to talk about what is similar and what is different to today.

Ask the children why the seaside is so popular now (good day out, fresh air, a place to play, nice change). Ask them why they think so many people wanted to go to the seaside in Victorian times (similar reasons, but stress the pollution of the air in cities in those times from coal fires and factories, plus a longer working week and shorter holidays).

Ideas for extension

Ask the children to design and produce a poster for the 1890s to attract people in towns like Manchester to visit Southport. Encourage them to think about the images to appear on the poster, and the main point that the text should make. One poster from 1900 said 'Healthy Southport – death rate only 13 per 1000' and it showed the promenade and the pier.

Ask the children to list the ways in which modern cars are better than those of the 1900s (they are safer, have cleaner exhausts, are more powerful, more comfortable, more reliable and have better headlights, steering and brakes).

Linked ICT activities

Tell the children that they are going to create a seaside postcard. Using a graphics program such as 'Dazzle', 'Fresco' or 'Granada Colours', show them how to use the paintbrush and the fill tools. Next show them how to paint a background for the postcard in the same way that they painted the weather scene in Chapter 8. They should save the background and start to add the items in the foreground.

Ask the children to decide whether they are going to create a postcard that shows a beach scene from the present or from the past. Show them how to add text to the postcard and how to change the font style, colour and size. Ask them to add a caption to the postcard, such as 'A day out in sunny Blackpool'.

Print out the final postcards and display them on a class display under the heading 'Wish you were here'.

Southport in 1890

Southport in 1890

Name _____

Past and present

Look at the pictures below. They show things at the seaside in the past. In the empty boxes, draw what the seaside looks like today.

Seaside past	Seaside now
Clothes	
Bathing machine	
Tram	
On the beach	

Name _____

Past and present

Look at the pictures below, which show things that were found at the seaside in the past.
In the empty boxes, draw what the seaside looks like today.

Seaside past	Seaside now

Name _____

Past and present

In the chart below, write a description of the seaside in the 1890s. Use the headings and Generic sheets 1 and 2 to help you.

Clothes	
Transport	
Getting around	
On the beach	
Other things	

On the back of this sheet, use the same headings to write about the seaside now.

Around the world

TEACHERS' NOTES

Children's experiences of seaside places outside the UK will vary considerably. This chapter encourages the use of a range of secondary sources to identify a variety of seaside places around the world.

Other seaside places

One starting point is to talk about why people choose to visit seaside places in other parts of the world rather than the UK. Seaside places abroad have all the attractions that UK seaside places have, namely:

- picturesque harbours and jetties
- fishing boats, still working and landing fresh fish and shellfish
- quaint coves
- beaches of sand or pebbles
- cliffs with caves, arches and stacks
- piers
- entertainments, such as video arcades
- hotels
- restaurants
- swimming pools
- golf courses
- opportunities for trips on ships and boats as well as water skiing and other water sports.

However, foreign seaside places may also have some or all of the following attractions:

- reliable fine sunny weather free from cloud cover or storms
- warm or hot temperatures
- different types of local food
- opportunities to eat and to sit outdoors in restaurants, hotels and apartments
- opportunities for activities such as swimming with dolphins or underwater diving to view coral reefs and exotic fish and other creatures
- opportunities to visit special places, such as the Blue Grotto in Malta or the Diamond Head in Hawaii.

However, it is also important to remember that seaside places abroad experience weather that can be dangerous. For example, Florida and places in the Caribbean have hurricanes in the August/September period.

Other natural hazards found at seaside places abroad include tsunamis. These are rare but may be the result of an underwater volcanic eruption or earthquake. These can do huge amounts of damage to coastal areas, especially in places where the land is flat and low-lying. Again, there is advice for visitors to these areas which consists mainly of listening to the local news and being ready to move to higher ground as quickly as possible if danger threatens.

Visitors to seaside places in the Mediterranean area may wonder why the tide does not rise and fall as it does in the rest of the world. This can be explained by the fact that the Mediterranean is an enclosed sea, with a very narrow entrance and exit at the Straits of Gibraltar. As a result there are no tides in the seaside places. This makes it easier to build hotels and apartments that come down very close to the water's edge because there is little danger of them being flooded by a very high tide.

Some seaside places abroad can be visited during the winter period in the UK. This is because they have a mild climate which means they stay warm during the winter. Places such as the South of France, Cyprus, Malta and the Canary Isles as well as the coast of North Africa all fall into this category.

Some seaside places abroad also have the attraction of offering visitors the chance to explore the remains of ancient civilisations. In countries such as Italy, Greece, Turkey, Egypt and Israel visitors can marvel at how people used to live in these seaside places many years ago.

Other seaside places abroad offer more exotic attractions, such as the chance to see the sand dunes of the Sahara desert and to ride on a camel in Egypt, Morocco or Tunisia. Other attractions include oases with palm trees and swimming pools together with the fruits from irrigated farming.

LESSON PLAN

Around the world

Geography objectives (Unit 4)
- To use secondary sources to find information.
- To develop awareness of the wider world.
- To learn about the nature of places.

Resources

- Generic sheets 1 and 2 (pages 98–99)
- Activity sheets 1–3 (pages 100–103)
- A map of Europe to include southern Spain

Starting points: *whole class*

Tell the children that they are going to look at seaside places outside the UK. Explain that they will look at the Costa del Sol. Tell them that the name means 'sunshine coast'. Ask questions such as:

- In which country is the Costa del Sol?
- Has anyone been there?
- What was it like?

Ask the children to imagine that they are going on holiday to the Costa del Sol. Use a question and answer technique to identify the five key things they need to know before deciding where to go.

Locate Spain on a map of the world and the Costa del Sol in the south.

Next show the children Generic sheet 1 on an OHP or in an enlarged version. Read the description of the region with the children. Use the map to locate the Costa del Sol and Malaga (where the main airport is). Then ask the children to read the description again in groups and to answer the five key questions below which should have been written on the board and read through with them.

- Where is this region? (It is in southern Spain on the Mediterranean coast.)
- When will we go? (What will the weather be like? Temperatures vary from 17°C to 30°C so we can go in winter or summer.)
- Why will we go? (What is there to do? A variety of things – water sports, trips to the mountains and lots of restaurants and cafes.)
- Where will we stay? (Hotel, self-catering,

camping? You could even stay in a flat in a high-rise block.)
- How will we get there? (By plane or by car and ferry? You can fly there from a local UK airport.)

Ask the children how a holiday in Malaga would be different from, or the same as, a seaside holiday in the UK. Use a question and answer technique to highlight some of the main differences and similarities as shown below. Write these under the headings.

	Things the same in Malaga and the UK	**Things different in Malaga**
Food	Fried food, hamburgers, chicken.	
Weather		Hot and sunny all summer. Warm in winter.
On the beach	Swimming, sunbathing, games (football, cricket), donkey rides, ice cream, fishing.	
Trips	Trips into the mountains, trips in fishing boats.	

Tell the children that they are now going to write postcards from the Costa del Sol to their friends.

Group activities

Activity sheet 1
This sheet is aimed at children who need more support. They need copies of Generic sheet 2. They are able to imagine that they are on holiday in the place shown in the picture. They have to draw a picture to show what they have been doing at the

resort. They should write the school address on the postcard.

Activity sheet 2

This sheet is aimed at children who can work independently. They have to write a description of what they have done on an imaginary holiday. They have to put the school address on the card. On the back of the sheet, they have to draw a picture of what they have been doing.

Activity sheet 3

This sheet is aimed at more able children. They are able to observe pictures and to write brief descriptions from one, imagining this was the view from their hotel window. They have to write a structured description of how they arrived in Malaga, what they can see and what they have been doing.

Plenary session

Share the responses to the activity sheets. Talk about things that the children could all do on a holiday in Malaga, such as swimming, playing on the beach and going on trips. Ask how the children could find out more about Malaga before they went (from holiday brochures, consulting newspapers for weather information or talking to people who have already been there). Make a list of secondary sources on the board as the children think of ideas.

Use examples from holiday brochures to look at the types of information we get about other seaside places, such as Malaysia, Hawaii or the Algarve in Portugal.

Ideas for support

Some children may need help with writing the postcard. So talk about the details shown in the picture on Generic sheet 1. Talk about what they could do (play on the beach, swim in a pool, play beach football, sail a boat); where they might stay (an apartment in a tall block near a pool); and where they might eat (outdoors, near the sea or a pool under a palm tree). They may also need a little help in writing the school address.

Make a collection of postcards from around the world and use these as the basis for a wall display on seaside places, at the centre of which is a large world map.

Make a collection of travel brochures which feature seaside places in different parts of the world. Again, locate the places on a world map and ask the children to say how the places are similar and how they are different.

Ideas for extension

Give the children weather information for a series of holiday places from a newspaper. Ask them to find the places on a world map and then plot them on a blank world outline map. Then ask them to devise a series of symbols to be used next to each place to indicate what the temperature and other conditions, such as rainfall, wind or clouds are like.

Ask the children to use satellite images of weather over Europe and/or the Mediterranean to link the pattern of clouds shown on the images with the weather descriptions for the places that they have just been studying.

Linked ICT activities

Talk with the children about going on holiday to hot places. Find out who has been on a holiday where the weather was hot and sunny all the time. Make a list of all the places the children have been to at home and abroad.

Talk about what it might be like to live in a hot country. Take in some travel brochures for them to use and make use of the internet to look at different places around the world. If you have a whiteboard these images would be a good point for discussion activities with the children.

Talk to the children about what they think they would need to take with them if they were going on holiday to a very hot country. Using a word processing program, tell the children that they have to write a list of all the things that they would need to take with them for this holiday, thinking about clothes, something to play with, the hot weather and so on. Print out the list. If there is room in the classroom to bring in a suitcase for a display area, pin the lists to the suitcase or create a wall display of a suitcase and pin the lists to the wall display. Bring in some items to place in the suitcase, such as sunglasses, suncream, T-shirts and so on, or warm winter wear.

Around the world

This is a map showing the Costa del Sol in Spain. Lots of people from the UK go there for their holidays. Why?

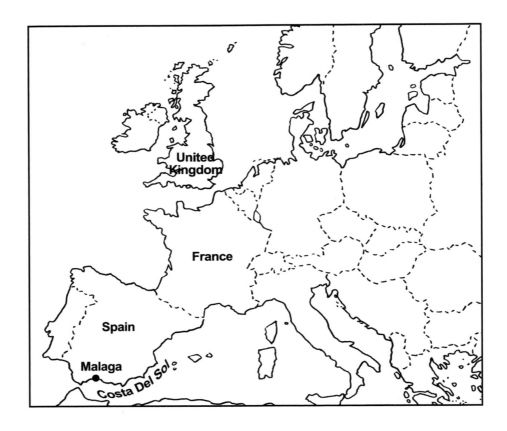

Southern Spain is sun-drenched and has always been popular. Temperatures in the day are 17ºC in January and 30ºC in July!

There are six hours of sunshine every day in January and in July this rises to twelve hours!

There are long, sandy beaches and behind them are dramatic mountains.

Enjoy sunbathing by the sea. There are lots of other things to do – from water sports, like water skiing or parasailing, to boat and yacht trips. Shops, cafes and bars attract people at night, together with a wide choice of nightclubs.

Stay in a luxury, high-rise apartment that overlooks the beach, at very reasonable prices.

There are direct flights to Malaga from most UK airports.

The Costa del Sol

Around the world

Look at the picture on Generic sheet 2.

Fill out the postcard below, telling your friends what you have done on holiday on the Costa del Sol. Draw a picture and write a sentence.
Then write the address of your school on the postcard.

Name _____

Around the world

You are on holiday on the Costa del Sol. This is the front of a postcard you are going to send.

This is the back of the postcard. Write to tell your friends what you have been doing. Put your school address on the card.

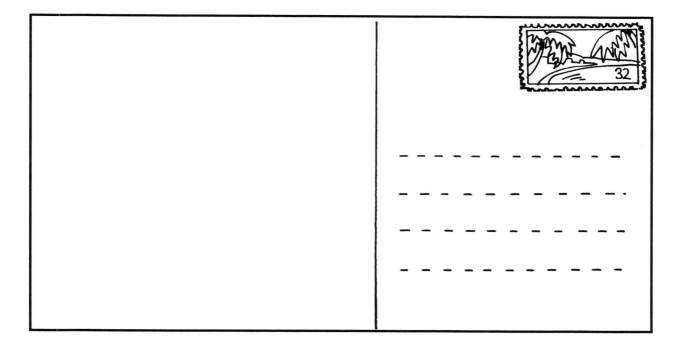

On the back of this sheet, draw a picture of one thing you have been doing on this holiday.

Name _____

Around the world

This is the view from your hotel window on the Costa del Sol.
Write to your friends on the postcard below saying:

- how you got here;
- what you can see from your bedroom window;
- what you have been doing.

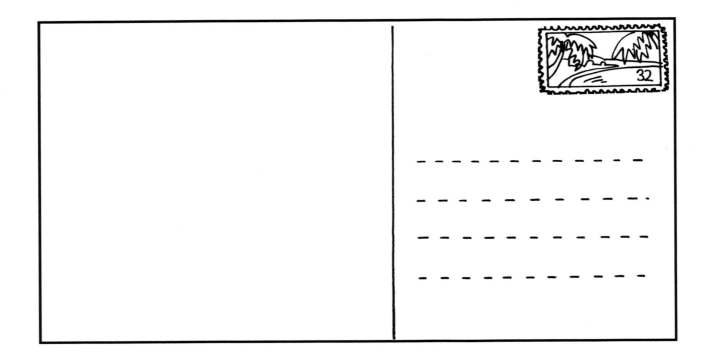

Resources

My World 2 for Windows, **Talking Write Away**,
Counter for Windows, **Fresco** and **Dazzle**
Granada Learning Semerc
Granada Television, Quay St, Manchester,
M60 9EA
Tel 0161 827 2927
http://www.shop.granada-learning.com/bin/venda

Textease
Softease Ltd
Textease 2000 (PC)
Market Place, Ashbourne, Derbyshire DE6 1ES
Tel 01335 343421
http://www.softease.com/textease.htm

Clicker 4
Crick Software Ltd
Crick House, Boarden Close, Moulton Park,
Northampton, NN3 6LF
Tel 01604 671691
www.cricksoft.com